THE POWER OF OUCH!

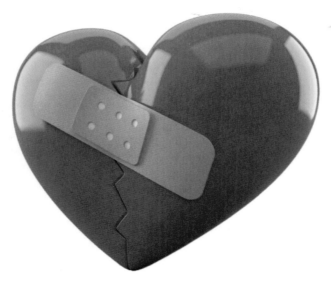

AN ILLUSTRATED GUIDE TO HEALING FROM HURT AND CREATING A LIFE OF LOVE & CONNECTION

SONDRA HARMON

This publication includes personal stories and anecdotes from the author's life, interviews and interactions with clients. It reflects the author's recollections of these experiences. Names and identifying characteristics of some individuals have been changed and some dialogue has been re-created from memory.

For information about special discounts for bulk purchases visit sondraharmon.com/thepowerofouch.

Graphic Images: Patrick Carlson

Photographs: Stefania Harangus

Typesetter: Zakirunissa Karthigeyan

Names: Sondra Harmon, author

Title: The Power of OUCH! - An illustrated guide to healing from hurt and creating a life of love & connection.

ISBN: 978-1-7358778-1-5

ISBN: 978-1-7358778-0-8

DEDICATION

This book is dedicated to Richard Harmon—my husband, my love, my Mitra—thank you for giving me a life filled with love, joy, and the freedom to just be myself. I am blessed beyond words to be sharing a life together.

ACKNOWLEDGEMENTS

I want to both thank and introduce the three women who helped me understand the power of saying OUCH!

Linda Chaé

Linda is an entrepreneur, award-winning business leader, and Founder and CEO of Chaé Organics. She is the magic behind so many of the popular skin and home care products sold today. More than that, she has been my friend and mentor for the last half-decade and has taught me everything she knows about the secrets of staying in a long-term, loving relationship.

Preethaji

Spiritual leader, guiding meditation retreats all over the world, best-selling author of the book, *The Four Sacred Secrets*, and Founder of O&O Academy in India, Preethaji has impacted the lives of millions of people around the world. I was blessed to study with her and her teachers at their campus in India and then support her events in the US. Her consciousness-expanding meditations have allowed me to see the beauty of life. Her invaluable pearls of wisdom and reflective meditations on relationships have given me the ability to be in relationships from a beautiful state of love and connection, rather than a suffering state of scarcity and fear. These meditations also allowed me to share that experience with others.

Alison Armstrong

Alison is a transformational teacher and author of the book, *The Queen's Code*. She founded PAX, a program that educates men and women about the predicament of gender, the interaction of masculinity and femininity, and the principles of the paradigm of partnership. Her book completely transformed how I relate to the men in my life, ultimately creating more harmony and peace.

After seeing what was possible, I wanted to learn from her directly. I spent two and a half years researching with Alison and teaching hundreds of people, becoming certified to teach her work.

These three women are at the core of my transformation, but there are numerous thought leaders whose works I have read, talks I have listened to, and seminars I have attended—my heartfelt thanks to all of them.

So Many OTHERS

First, were all the many people who participated in my interviews, giving me honest and authentic stories to share in my workshops and in this book. Also, a big thank you to all the many friends and family who supported me with feedback and encouragement, especially **Angie Maserati** (who recorded all the audio files to help you) and the rest of the gals from **The Cool Chick Café**.

I need to give a special thank you to **Brendon Burchard**, who first planted the seed that authoring a book was attainable and provided so much support through his own books, videos and High Performance Mastermind.

Next, I must thank **Nikki Zimbler.** She was not just my developmental editor; but also cheerleader, therapist and coach. Without her guidance and support, I would have never completed this book. She gave me focus and kept me from deleting the whole book on several occasions. Huggles, my mate.

Lastly, without my husband, I would not have known how loving a relationship could be. And I would not have become so determined to share what I've learned with others. Thank you, **Richard Harmon**, for this beautiful life.

TABLE OF CONTENTS

PART 1

THE POWER OF OUCH!

PART ONE

1

PACK YOUR BAGS—
WE'RE OFF!

We all want connection in our lives and in our relationships; to experience the joy of being fully alive in the moment and attuned to others. We want to feel seen and heard, respected, and appreciated, and most importantly, loved.

It doesn't have to be in the context of a romantic relationship (though often it is). We want, crave, and *need* connection with our family, our friends, our community, with life in general, and even with ourselves.

Growing up, I only experienced that type of connection in drips and dribbles. Initially, I could find it easily enough, but then, almost inevitably, it slipped through my fingers. It was like I was a sieve, and the love just kept pouring out through all the tiny holes in me. And no matter how fast I tried to plug up those holes, the love would never stay. I would feel it leak out and ebb away, and there was seemingly nothing I could do about it.

So, I convinced myself that I didn't need connection and shouldn't really expect love. I hid behind the mask of, "I'm doing great!" What a delusion!

The truth is, I didn't know *how* to stay connected. I didn't know what to do in those inevitable moments of disconnection, hurt, upset, and disappointment because I didn't know how to say OUCH! to others or myself.

This book is part autobiography and part guidebook, as I lead you down the exact path I took from misery in my relationships to pure, resounding joy. I now take others on this journey, both in workshops and with private clients, am so excited to share this path to creating more love and connection in your life.

I want to reiterate that this isn't just about romantic relationships. We can (and often do) get hurt, disrespected, disappointed, and upset in any relationship. It can be with our parents, our children, our friends and colleagues, and even ourselves. *The Power of OUCH!* can transform all these relationships.

But, if you picked this book up wanting to know how to keep people from hurting your feelings, crushing your spirit, devaluing your worth, or simply disappointing or annoying you—you might as well put it straight back down.

So many books about relationships start with the promise of, "If you do this, then they will do that." This book is NOT about ways to get your partner, family, friends, or colleagues to treat you differently, love you more, or change themselves in any way.

You might also be thinking that if you could "fix" yourself, then it would "fix" your relationships, and keep you from getting hurt. While there are plenty of books to teach you how to pick the right words or use correct body language or think positive thoughts, as you might have guessed, this book is NOT one of them.

Simply put, this is about healing the inevitable hurt and disappointment you will feel and allow you to stay connected and experiencing love.

During our time together, we are going to examine everything we are taught about hurt and turn it completely on its head, and we're going to do it in a way that creates more connection (with yourself and others) and more love (for life and the people in it). That being said, I'm not going to preach to you about what you should or shouldn't DO. Instead, we are simply going to become aware of and examine mental landmines that can become our downfall.

Awareness, in and of itself, has the power to change everything. It certainly did for me. Let me explain how I came to realize this.

Business was always easy for me. I could form solid, trustworthy relationships with clients and colleagues with relative ease. But that wasn't the case with most of my personal relationships, especially romantic ones.

My experience in my first three long-term relationships (lasting 8–10 years each) was very much like the fairytale, *Goldilocks*. The first was too hard, the second too soft, and the third—which was supposed to be just right—felt worse than the first two combined.

A shift finally happened for me when I met a woman named Linda Chaé. In keeping with the fairytale metaphor, if I were Cinderella, Linda would be my Fairy Godmother.

I first met Linda, Founder and CEO of Chaé Organics, at a conference where she was the keynote speaker. After listening to her talk, I saw her in the hallway holding hands with her CFO, Frank Maggio. Though they were both in their mid-60s, they gazed at each other like lovestruck teenagers. It was utterly adorable.

As I watched from afar, I created a whole backstory about the smitten pair. Frank was a widower, and Linda was only recently divorced. They met late in life, and were now in the first stages of dating—*How sweet!* Confident in my assumptions, I knew I had their entire relationship all figured out. How wrong I was!

Frank and Linda had been married for over thirty-five years, yet they looked and behaved like newlyweds. *How could that be?* I was fascinated.

I spent several days with them, both at their manufacturing facilities and in their home, and it was clear they were genuinely still smitten after all that time. One day, during a three-hour drive with Frank, he spent the entire drive telling me how amazing his wife was. It hardly seemed possible, and I desperately wanted to know what she knew about the key to maintaining a long-term, happy relationship.

A few days later, over a glass (okay . . . *two* glasses) of wine, I told Linda my story and expressed my suffering, both the past and the present. I shared things that had been bottled up for so long, feelings that I'd never before told a stranger (and rarely even friends). As I stared into my glass of red wine, sobbing, Linda asked me, "Sweetie, what's in it for you?"

I stopped mid-sob, and looked inward. It was the first time I became curious about my own inner experience and thoughts, and it was the last time I ever cried like that. With one question, Linda made me realize I'd been going about this all wrong.

Linda's question—"Sweetie, what's in it for you?"—took me on a marvelous, insightful, almost magical journey of self-awareness.

First, I went to India to study with enlightened sages learning ancient wisdoms. Next, I traveled all around the U.S., studying intensively for over two years with one of the foremost transformational leaders in relationships. But most importantly, I took an inquisitive look at my own motivations and methods.

I want to take you on a tour of what I learned, where I'll be playing the role of your Tour Guide. Through this tour, I'm going to share my insights and inquiries to help you keep connected, loving relationships.

Oh ... and if you are wondering where my path has led me so far, I met a wonderful, kind, caring, beautiful man that I married and with whom I now share endless joy, laughter, and love.

As your Tour Guide, let me tell you a bit about where we are going to travel together in the forthcoming chapters. We are going to explore using images, personal stories, and examples to illustrate the most crucial points.

There are numerous **Observation Breaks** that are the core of this journey. Please take the time—as much time as needed—to read, reflect, and answer each of the questions in these sections. There are a few ways I recommend doing this:

1. Use them as journal prompts. Simply use a piece of paper and write your answers, or download and print the worksheets that are available at the Online Resources, which can be found at www.sondraharmon.com/OUCH. I'll discuss more about these resources in a moment.
2. Pair up with someone else as a "Travel Buddy" and take turns answering and listening.
3. Join or create a book club and take turns going around the room.
4. Simply read a question, close your eyes, take a deep breath, and look at the answers you see in your mind. Make sure to be in a comfortable, safe place when doing this.

During the Observation Breaks, it's helpful to simply notice the examples and answers that come to mind, without trying to analyze, relive, or explain anything.

In addition, there are **Turning Points** throughout the book. In any journey, you need to have the freedom to say, "I want to stop." A friend of mine and his son wanted to climb Mt.

Kilimanjaro. They got all the way there after months of planning and training, only to decide to turn back after his son wasn't feeling well. The next year they went back and climbed to the summit. Climbing when they weren't ready would have been miserable.

So, whenever you come to a **Turning Point** and don't want to go further, don't. Put the book aside and either come back to it later, or—if you decide this isn't the journey for you—you can write to me for a refund.

As your Tour Guide, I'll be taking you to three locations—or parts—to explore.

The first part of the book covers how we connect and how we disconnect.

The second part covers a way to release the pain we are holding on to.

The third part is about making life less OUCHY! This section requires more work, and includes exercises and explorations into areas of your mind you might not have noticed before. You'll want to set aside uninterrupted time to complete them.

Important Note: This book is based on an in-person, one-day workshop I lead. There are some things that were hard to translate into a book, so I have created an online resource area with worksheets, videos, additional notes and links to references that will help you have a fuller experience. You can access it here: www.sondraharmon.com/ouch. I'll be referring to it throughout the book as the **Online Resources**.

I also love to connect with my readers, so please feel free to write to me anytime: me@sondraharmon.com.

2

CONNECTION AND DISCONNECTION

Humans are social creatures. Sure, we like to be alone sometimes, but not in the "I-feel-ALL-alone" way of being alone. Studies have shown that a lack of social connection heightens health risks as much as smoking fifteen cigarettes a day.

I like to remind people that connection is easy. Taking down the walls we put up to prevent it? *That* is hard. Look at little kids on a playground or the beach. They automatically forge a friendship.

I was struck, once, by how naturally this happens as I waited to board my flight at an airport. All the adults were either engrossed in their books or papers or they were "people watching," like me. Two toddlers from different families and different races were sitting across the aisle from each other. After no more than five minutes, they were holding hands and running up and down the terminal. Their laughter filled the entire area. As adults, it's not so easy—though how we wish it were!

I bring this up because it wouldn't be worth coming on this journey with me if we didn't know or remember the joy of pure connection. There are two exercises to accomplish this.

The first is a twenty-minute exercise I do in my workshops. It involves finding a willing partner to work with (or you can log into the Online Resources to find someone else to pair up with). If you don't want to stop reading, or don't have a willing and curious acquaintance, I offer an Alternate Connection Exercise, instead.

Exercise #1—Connection

This is based on Mandy Len Catron's essay "To Fall in Love with Anyone, Do This". The article talks about a 1997 study conducted by psychologist Arthur Aron, in which he compiled a list of 36 questions to see if intimacy and connection could be established more quickly if each person honestly and openly answered each question. He found that not only did it work effectively, but that it also helped those in long-term relationships to rekindle and reconnect in ways he never expected.

Just a side story, around the time my husband, Richard, and I first started dating, I saw this article and really wanted to try it out with the next person that piqued my interest. I was super shy about it all and said something to the effect of, "There's this thing that I'd like to try with you to help us get to know each other," to which he replied, "Sure, then after that I also have a thing I'd like to try." And as you may have guessed, we were both talking about the same "thing"! We spent hours asking, answering, and sharing; it was fun, insightful, and it was truly connecting.

The exercise you're about to do is an abbreviated version of the 36 questions, using just four of them.

Spend two minutes a piece answering each question. Alternate who starts first.

1. What is the greatest accomplishment of your life, and how did that make you feel?
2. Is there something that you've dreamed of doing for a long time, and why haven't you done it?
3. If you knew that you were going to die suddenly in a year's time, is there anything you would change about the way you are now living, and if so, why?
4. If you were to die this evening with no opportunity to communicate with anyone, what would you most regret not having told someone? Why haven't you told them yet?

After completion, look into one another's eyes for two full minutes.

Discuss how you both feel having completed the exercise. Do you feel more connected?

Exercise #2—Alternative

You will need to close your eyes for this one. There are three steps that you will do three times. There is an audio file at the Online Resources if you would prefer to listen to prompts.

- Close your eyes.
- Remember a moment in which you were very connected with someone (it can be a friend, family member, romantic

partner, stranger, even a pet)

- Imagine that moment is happening right now.
- Spend several minutes noticing everything about how you feel, both your body and your emotions.
- Now smile at that memory.
- Do this two more times with different moments of connection.

Observation Break

Describe how connection feels to you.

What would feeling like this more of the time allow you to **be**?

What would feeling like this more of the time allow you to **do**?

What would feeling like this more of the time allow you to **have**?

TURNING POINT: Do you want more connection in your life? If yes, read on.

In addition to noticing the ways we connect, it is also important to bring awareness to how we disconnect. The mechanisms of disconnection are pretty simple.

Something happens or is said that you didn't expect and didn't want. Or, something *doesn't* happen or *isn't* said that you expected and wanted.

It hurts, either a lot or a little. Either way, it feels, as my friend Jessica says, "Yucky." It creates tension in your body and includes an accompanying emotion.

For example:

- A colleague is late for an important meeting.
- A new romantic interest doesn't text you the next morning after a date.
- Your mother doesn't call you on your birthday.
- A friend loses their temper with you.
- The line at the bank is soooooo long.
- Your husband is looking at his phone rather than paying attention to you.

All of these can create tension. There was something you wanted or didn't want. Notice that something was or wasn't said, or something was or wasn't done, and it didn't match up with what you thought would happen. OUCH!

Let's see if this is true for you.

Observation Break

What is something that has upset you, hurt your feelings, or simply disappointed you that is still causing tension?

What did you want or expect to happen or not happen in that circumstance?

3

SAYING OUCH!

In the physical world, if you stub your toe on a table, you are likely to say, "Ooooo!" or "Oww!" or "OUCH!" More often than not, we do it instinctively.

My friend Jessica and I were on the beach one time, when she was stung by a bee. She's the sweetest gal I know, so imagine my shock when the words that came out of her mouth were, "OUCH! FUCK!! Motherfucker! OWWWW!"

In a true OUCH!, there is no blame, only pain. In the seconds after you stub your toe, it doesn't matter if the table was where it shouldn't have been or your foot was in a place it shouldn't have been. Or with Jessica, it doesn't matter if it wasn't a bee that stung her and it was actually a hornet. The end result was pain, and the expression of this pain is "OUCH!" or one of its relatives.

If others are around you, they might say something like, "Are you okay? What can I do to help?" If they were involved, they might say, "Oh, I'm so sorry!" Again, this is something that happens naturally.

If you stub your toe, you let the pain work its way out of your body. You check your foot and rub it, massaging it until it feels better. You might put ice on it. You might bandage it if it starts to bleed. You might just rest it, propping your foot on a pillow, or if it's bad, you might decide that you need help from a doctor. All these things are designed to tend to the pain.

And while you are still in pain, you are probably not going to start rearranging furniture or ordering more protective shoes. Instinctively, you handle the pain first.

But **we so rarely do this in relationships**. We hold onto the pain, we hold onto the tension, and we suppress the OUCH!

So, let's look at the definition of the word itself. This is from the Merriam-Webster's dictionary:

Ouch: interjection; used especially to express sudden pain

OUCH! can get a bad rap because people think saying it is a way of focusing on the negative. I think saying OUCH! is great! Considering the title of this book, you might have already guessed that.

Some might ask, "Isn't that the opposite of everything we are taught about positive thinking and its benefits? Aren't you supposed to just focus on the good? Doesn't energy flow where attention goes?" Focusing on the beauty in life, having gratitude and living in a beautiful state is, for sure, a way to approach life; but it doesn't mean ignoring our pains or pushing them away, because if we do that, we stay unconsciously attached to the hurt.

If there is a hurt in your life, think of it as stuck energy. It's not flowing, causing it to pool inside you like stagnant water. Bringing conscious awareness to that stuck point allows it to drain, leaving you with space for new experiences to replace it.

In the following chapters, I'll be asking you to truly see and experience the power of OUCH!

The observations and exercises provided will uncover the unconscious ways we hold onto hurt and how we are continually creating more.

It gives you a path to embrace ALL your experiences instead of pushing parts of yourself away. It gives you more attention and energy to spend on the things you **do** want to create, allowing you to have more of those beautiful moments of connection.

If this seems scary, don't worry. Looking at ancient battle sites, spooky burial grounds, or even abandoned ghost towns and fully viewing them through the eyes of curiosity, compassion, and love can be a wondrous adventure. Plus, I'm here as your Tour Guide; I've personally "been there and done that."

TURNING POINT: Are you ready to start with the incredible power of saying ouch!?

YAY! Let the journey begin!

The first time I heard about the power of OUCH! was from Linda, my Fairy Godmother. (Remember her from the first chapter?)

Prior to meeting Linda, I couldn't remember ever having said "OUCH!" out loud or even to myself. Up until that point, my OUCH! equivalents were really only questions like, "What's wrong with me?" or "What's wrong with them?"

I learned so many things from Linda, but one of the first and most profound was to actually say "OUCH!"

The way she described it, when Frank did something to hurt her feelings, it hurt and it felt "Ouchy," so that is what she said. She would even shake her hands from side to side in front of her as she said it (I have a rare video of her teaching this topic on the OUCH! Online Resources so you can see it for yourself). In case you are wondering, she hadn't always said OUCH! It was only after years of marriage that she discovered how helpful it was. As for me, I was lucky Linda taught me this invaluable lesson, and I want to share this lesson with you now.

When people use the word OUCH!, it doesn't have to be that exact word every time. Some people I interviewed, like Linda, say exactly that. Others gave me great alternatives. One woman made a pouty sort of sound "Humph" that had no actual word attached to it. One wonderful woman said she hisses just like a cat. Another says, "Ouchy!" I say "Daa!" (Don't ask me why, I have no idea, but it's what I say).

None of these is anything but a vocal expression of how we feel. And it might be different sounds for different experiences. Hurt feelings might sound like "Ooow!" Disrespect might sound like "Damn!" Disappointment might sound like "Awwww" or "Yikes." Annoyance might sound like "Tsk!" and so on.

Observation Break

What words do you use or what sounds do you make when you have been hurt physically? Say these out loud right now, if you feel comfortable, and do the same for the following questions too.

What words do you use or sounds do you make when someone hurts your feelings?

What words do you use or sounds do you make when someone disrespects you?

What words do you use or sounds do you make when someone annoys you?

What words do you use or sounds do you make when someone disappoints you?

See how different they all are!

Let's take a deeper look at OUCH! It is an interjection. This isn't meant to be a grammar lesson, but I want to make sure we are on the same page for some of the key words we will be using along our journey.

What is an interjection? Here is what the dictionary has to say:

"We use interjections to express emotions such as pleasure, surprise, shock, and disgust. Most interjections are just sounds, rather than actual words, and come at the beginning or at the end of what we say. Interjections are more common in speaking than in writing."

Throughout this book, please remember that when I'm using the word OUCH!, it is an interjection. It is simply an expression of emotion, and probably just a sound with a lot of emotion attached to it.

I don't know about you, but I grew up watching *Schoolhouse Rock*, a series of short cartoons designed to teach children about grammar and history with songs and cute characters.

Forty-five years after first watching this, I can still sing their song *Interjections!* You are all so very lucky this is a book and not one of my live workshops where I am prone to breaking out into song. The original video is still online—just google "Schoolhouse Rock Interjections" or you can get the link on the Resources Page.

Other people I interviewed regarding what they say when they experience hurt give examples such as:

"I don't like what you just did to me."

"Why did you do that?"

"That wasn't very nice.

"What's wrong with you?"

These may all be very important conversations to have, but when I say, "Say OUCH!" I really do mean that sound you make immediately after experiencing physical or mental pain.

If you convey a request or a criticism, it is definitely NOT an OUCH! Instead, it's an attempt to change something or someone. Even if you say, "You hurt my feelings," it's NOT an OUCH! either. So, let me stress this again, **OUCH! is simply a sound or word expressing pain**.

So often, we get hurt and we stay silent, we let it build up inside us, and we blame ourselves or others. There are so many things we do rather than simply saying "OUCH!" and letting the emotional pain dissolve from our minds and bodies. By stopping this flow, we are creating mini-PTSD episodes for ourselves every time we do it.

Note: This is a book about improving our day-to-day relationships, not dealing with severe physical or psychological trauma. If this book is bringing up moments of trauma or PTSD, please get effective, empathic help. If you don't know a professional, you can go to my Online Resources for a list of people I recommend.

In the book, *The Body Keeps Score*, the author Bessel van der Kolk says, "Immobilization keeps the body in a state of inescapable shock and learned helplessness."

So, while freaking out upon hearing that your in-laws are coming to visit for a week might not seem like a life-threatening situation, standing there silently and immobilized without even saying OUCH! is keeping the trauma alive.

By holding in all your natural responses, and not expressing yourself, you don't allow the pain to dissipate.

Oftentimes, we don't *want* to say OUCH! Here are some thoughts people have shared with me over the years:

- I don't want to say OUCH! because I don't want to seem like I'm causing trouble.
- I don't want to be too high maintenance.
- I don't want to say OUCH! because that would mean I'm vulnerable.
- I don't want anyone to know that they can hurt me.
- I don't want to bring anyone down in the moment, especially if other people are around.
- It's not a big deal.
- I'm a positive person and don't have time for any negatives.
- I want to refrain from saying OUCH! until something big happens. Tiny things aren't important enough to bring up at the moment.

- I don't know what others would think of me.
- It isn't the right time or place to speak.
- They might think I don't like them, or there is something wrong with the relationship.
- I would be saying OUCH! all the time. People wouldn't want to hang out with me.
- I don't know how they will react. They could react badly.
- I don't want to start a battle.

If you look at all these statements, they either fall into the *Being Accepted* category or *Being in Control*. Or a bit of both.

But here is something very, very important. **Saying OUCH! isn't for anyone else**. It isn't to influence anyone else; it isn't to change anyone else. **It is 100% for you**. It is a tool for you to bring focus and compassion to your pain so you can heal. It actually helps to release the pain, especially if there is movement involved, such as shaking your arms or holding your heart.

Remember, OUCH! is simply an interjection. It says, "I'm in pain," the same way saying "Brrrrr!" says, "I'm cold."

If you are having any thoughts like, "I do say OUCH! all the time, I even cry, and they still DON'T change," I want to remind you, this isn't the purpose of saying OUCH! Yes, it lets someone know they are hurting you, and that person may change, but using OUCH! to create change for another isn't any more effective than saying OUCH! when you stub your toe in an attempt to get the table leg to stop being so hard. If you say OUCH! and expect a reaction from them, there may even be a second upset that follows when they don't react to you saying OUCH! the way you wanted or expected.

Let me give you a personal example. One fall day, I was walking with a date near a breezy lake. I felt cold. I instinctively said, "Brrrrr," as a wind gust came over the lake. Then I added, "Ooh, it's really cold outside." His immediate reaction was, "But it's not cold!"

How could he argue with me about something so obvious as a wind chill that was making me uncomfortable? Why wasn't he trying to help me? Had I just stopped at "Brrrrr," rather than adding in my judgment, we might not have argued. I could have said, "I feel cold," or even "I'm shivering," but "It's cold out" is a judgment and opinion, and it didn't match his. So, it became a disagreement. The disagreement was compounded again because I expected him to offer me his jacket in response. *Yikes!*

"Brrrrr!" simply meant I was feeling cold at that particular moment. If there is one thing you can be certain about, it is your own personal experience of things.

If you feel cold, you feel cold. If you feel hot, you feel hot. If you feel pain, you feel pain. Period.

Even if he had still said, "But it's not cold," it wouldn't matter. When I say "Brrrrr," or "I feel cold," I am only expressing my experience. The only person who can be 100% certain of my own experience is me, and that's NOT open for debate.

Observation Break

Notice the times you have felt hurt, disrespected, or disappointed, and you didn't react with a simple OUCH!

What do you think would have happened if you had said OUCH?

Are those thoughts centered around not being accepted or liked?

Are those thoughts centered around wanting to control the relationship or the other person or an outcome?

Are those thoughts centered on how you might be judged?

How many times this week did someone do something that hurt your feelings, even a little?

How many times this week did someone do something that was disrespectful, annoying, or disappointing?

Have you ever questioned your experience, saying to yourself, "I shouldn't feel this way," or "That's not a good response," or "I'm too sensitive"? What did your thoughts sound like?

Future Observations

Over the next few days, start looking for these times when you feel hurt, disrespected, or disappointed, and you don't say anything out loud.

Try imagining yourself saying OUCH!

Also, notice if you have any judgments of any kind.

The second woman who taught me about OUCH! was Alison Armstrong in her book, *The Queen's Code.*

In the book, one of the characters, Claudia, talks about saying "OUCH!" She is sort of the fictional version of my real-life Linda. Claudia says, "When I am hurt, I speak up and I can be healed." She then adds, "We assume people know when they have hurt us and that they do not care enough to heal us. More often, folks are unaware of what they have done." How easily we forget that others can't read our minds.

Not saying OUCH! keeps others from even knowing you are hurt and from helping you heal from the hurt. Again, I want to stress that you don't say OUCH! in order to get others to do anything. But you take away their ability to choose how to respond when you don't say you are hurting.

Also, remember it helps to say OUCH! without adding an opinion to it. When you say things like, "OUCH! You shouldn't do that!" or "OUCH! What's wrong with you?!" or "OUCH! You are hateful!" you are creating potential hurts for the other person.

I know about the immense power of saying OUCH! from my personal experience and the experiences of others I've interviewed, but there are also studies on this. The general theory is that saying OUCH! can reduce pain.

At the Online Resources, there is a study where they looked at this very idea. The study concludes that "These results provide the first evidence that vocalizing helps individuals cope with pain."

Are You Willing to Say OUCH?

Saying OUCH! and tending to your hurt takes courage and effort. And it goes against so many things we are taught:

- "Big girls don't cry."
- "Never let them see you sweat."
- "Don't be sad."
- "Stop being a baby."
- "Don't show your weakness."

These are mine, but you probably have your own list of things you were told throughout your life that you shouldn't do.

What we are never really told is what to do instead. What should we do with the hurt, anger, frustration, or terror? Wouldn't it be nice to learn ways to dissolve it or grow from it?

Even reading this book up to this point took effort, time, and resources. What is the payoff you are hoping for?

TURNING POINT: Do you want to learn a new way of doing this? If yes, read on.

Think back to the Connection Exercise in Chapter 2, in which you asked and answered four of the 36 Questions, and remember what connection feels like and how easy it was.

Clients sometimes argue that it takes two to feel connected, telling me, "When my husband is yelling at me, he is the one causing the disconnection, not me." But this is simply not the case. It may take two to tango, but it only takes one to maintain a connection. There is a beautiful video on the internet showing a father staying connected with his two-year-old daughter as she throws a temper tantrum, hitting and kicking and crying. If you want to check it out, it is in the Online Resources.

We don't ever have to feel disconnected, and we don't have to continue to be hurt—unless we choose to. Often though, this choice isn't made consciously. In the first part of the book, we covered connection and disconnection. I hope you saw that it really isn't that hard to connect.

Important side note: I am often asked, "Does this mean I need to stay in relationships that are damaging to me?" Absolutely not!!!

However, the person you most often need to connect with, the person you stopped paying attention to, is YOU.

But, back to OUCH! Both the outward vocalization and the

exercises in this book have the ability to free you from hurt, allowing you to both experience and respond to life from a different state *and* respond to yourself and the people in your life from a state of connection, not disconnection.

The trick isn't in connecting; it's in NOT disconnecting.

And this is where OUCH! comes in.

But we don't say OUCH! So, if we are NOT saying OUCH! and caring for our hurt, what ARE we doing instead?

This next section covers some of the most common things that occur when you don't say OUCH! and allow the tension to dissipate. Because when we don't do that, we end up ruminating about it for hours, days, weeks, or even years—and that's when things start to go downhill, in a very disconnecting way.

4

INTRODUCTION TO
HOT POTATOES

I love metaphors. So, let's say life hands you a "Hot Potato." In the physical world, if you pick up a hot potato or try to eat a hot potato, you'll more than likely say, "OUCH!," the magic word we are talking about. But with our "hot emotions," we don't tend to do that.

So, let's look at how I'm using the term "Hot Potato." Here's my favorite definition: "**a situation or subject that people disagree strongly about and that no one wants to deal with.**"

Here are some examples of a Hot Potato:

You get fired, OUCH!— Hot Potato

Your partner leaves you, OUCH!—Hot Potato

Someone cuts you off in traffic, OUCH!—Hot Potato

Your new phone got lost in the mail, OUCH!—Hot Potato

All of the above are things you disagree with and don't want. When you want something and don't get it, or get something that you don't want, it creates tension. You are pulling one way, and reality is pulling in the opposite direction—tension.

In relationships, the examples are limitless. Below is a short list.

Being any of the following:

- Ignored
- Unappreciated
- Unloved
- Unseen
- Rejected
- Judged
- Dismissed
- Disregarded
- Disrespected
- Belittled
- Endangered
- Threatened
- Heartbroken
- Blocked
- Disappointed
- Betrayed
- Ridiculed
- Misled
- Misunderstood
- Bullied

There are so many more examples, but hopefully, you get the gist.

What are other one-word examples of Hot Potatoes that come to mind for you?

Hot Potatoes in life often involve surprise or something unexpected and are usually sudden.

Here's something fun to help you remember to look for the Hot Potatoes. Again, you are so lucky this is a book, and I can't actually sing this to you, but there is a song about Hot Potatoes that would be fun for you to watch now. It is called, surprise, surprise, the *Hot Potato Song* by The Wiggles, and is most definitely a children's song. This one has zero educational purpose, as far as I can tell. When I discovered it while creating my first workshop, I couldn't get it out of my head. My husband begged me to stop singing it . . . definitely a Hot Potato on his part. This catchy tune is at the Online Resources.

Before we move on, let's take a look at how expectation and suddenness play a major role. Let's start with the example of getting cut off by another car in traffic. You instantly foresee an accident. You get tense—Hot Potato. If the person moving over had given you plenty of warning with a turn signal well in advance, and maybe even waited for you to give them room to move over, it would have been a more pleasant sensation.

At a basic level, it also creates tension in our bodies when this happens. It can be tension as a result of experiencing something we perceive as a threat, or bad, or unwanted, or sometimes wanting to experience something we feel is crucial, needed, or imperative.

Let's look at where that tension lives and how it relates to survival instincts.

My favorite definition of instinct is: "A primal biological urge compelling response in order to relieve tension."

First of all, it's primal, something primitive, primary, or fundamental, so coming before all this other stuff. The basics having to do with survival.

It's biological, having to do with living organisms. It's about our bodies. We feel hungry, so when we see a restaurant, we want to stop and eat. We feel cold, so we want to turn up the heat.

Instinct drives us to release tension. It triggers something in our bodies that compels us to react.

For example, when I look over a balcony up in one of the skyscrapers in NYC to the streets below, my stomach feels like I have worms wriggling around in it. I want to move away from the balcony. Maybe the same happens to you. It's instinct. Look at the logic of that. When humans lived, not in high-rises, but jungles, it would be good to have bodies with warning systems to keep us from falling.

If I were creating bodies that I wanted to survive, I would probably put in an automatic sensor so the bodies would notice when they are too close to the edge of something high, compelling them to move away. And in fact, I'm sure the Roomba robot vacuum we got my mom for Christmas has this feature to keep it from hurtling down the stairs.

Funny enough, one time, wanting to take a picture of the Statue of Liberty from the Staten Island Ferry, I held my iPhone out over a railing, and I got the exact same sickening feeling in my stomach.

I'm not the only one. A couple of days after I noticed this, I demonstrated it in a workshop. The room we were in was on the 30th-floor and when I put my iPhone out over the balcony, one of the women actually physically reacted. She backed away, doubled over, and couldn't even watch me dangle my phone above the streets of Manhattan.

She, like me, felt a physical reaction for something only modern meanings could create. If you were a caveman or cavewoman, holding a tiny slab of glass and metal over a cliff would have zero meaning. In fact, you might intentionally throw it over the cliff, not wanting some strange, beeping, foreign object in your possession. But, if that same cavewoman held her baby over the cliff, I'm pretty sure she would have a huge "danger, danger" warning in her body.

Often in relationships, rather than recognizing and releasing where the tension is coming from and then moving towards your goal (as I did with my phone to get that picture of the Statue of Liberty), we unconsciously handle these Hot Potatoes in ways that contribute to disconnection and hurt.

HOW WE HANDLE HOT POTATOES

The next several chapters are going to cover the many things we do that keep the tension (i.e., our Hot Potatoes) burning. I'll be using lots of stories, examples, and cartoons to make things as clear as possible. We'll also look at the positives and negatives of handling each "Hot Potato" in sections called **Why It's Awesome** and **Why It's Not**.

Remember at the beginning of this book when I said it isn't about changing you at all? This is simply a way to bring awareness to the pluses and minuses of what we do in relationships when we get this tension.

We're about to explore the most common ways that we handle Hot Potatoes. Let's start with my personal favorite . . .

5

SWEEP IT UNDER THE RUG

One way we deal with Hot Potatoes is by ignoring them completely or pretending they don't exist—essentially sweeping them under the rug. We say, "Hot Potato? Oh no, I don't have a Hot Potato. Nope, no Hot Potatoes here."

The first couple of times, especially in relationships, it's easy to ignore them. By ignore, I don't mean healing the hurt or letting go of the tension. I mean keeping the Hot Potatoes while TRYING to ignore them. Pretending, to yourself and those around you, that everything is totally fine. But, of course, you know it's not.

There was something I carried with me for years and years and years with my former husband. We were getting ready to go on our first trip together as a couple, to Florida then to the British Virgin Islands. We boarded the plane for our domestic flight, using our driving licenses as ID, and as we sat in our seats, he realized he had left his passport at home, which we'd need for the flight to the BVI. Then, he started berating ME for not reminding HIM to bring his passport. How could that even

be??!!! How could that happen??!!! What a jerk this new man in my life was. Notice, I never said OUCH!

I never openly and honestly told him the effect it had on me. We were together for ten years and I never let it go, and I never told him. Well, that is until I started using this as an example in my workshops. As I was writing this book, I called him to chat about that moment. He didn't even remember it ever happened. How often has that happened to you, where a hurtful incident occurs in your life and the other person has no recollection of it—and vice versa?

I hear it all the time with clients. They will say, "There were red flags" from years ago. Then with every subsequent argument, they will keep going back to that first hurt, even though the other party might not even know of its existence.

As for its impact on others, so many people get blindsided. Seen from the other side, it looks like this: a man I interviewed told me a story about his wife. They had been married for years. He was completely in love with her, and from his perspective, did everything he could to be a good husband and father. They went to an event, and at one point, the speaker started talking about relationships. Without warning, his wife stormed out, obviously upset about something. He was in shock, thinking there was nothing wrong between them, and assumed someone else must have said something to upset her.

He followed her out and through her tears, the reason flooded out of her. When they had first married seventeen years ago, they'd lived with his family for a while. As a new bride, she felt he'd taken his mother's side over hers on several occasions. She'd felt unsupported and unloved, with a little bit of betrayal thrown in for good measure, and she'd held onto that feeling for nearly two decades.

The first few potatoes we can just drop or cool while there aren't too many of them. The problem is, when the pile is up to your eyeballs, or when the underlying burden becomes so strong, you are already buried. Your Hot Potato pile keeps growing and growing, and pretty soon you can't move under the sheer weight of it, and when

you can't move, you get stuck. Then, either you explode about even the smallest of things or you slowly burn away, compressed under the immense weight and intense heat.

For some people, it can feel suffocating; for others it can feel like a deep underlying current of sadness or anger. For most people, it becomes overwhelming.

Why It's Awesome

One of the key points about Hot Potatoes is they are unexpected. They are surprising. Sometimes you feel you don't have the time or aren't in the right place to deal with a Hot Potato. If you don't want to say OUCH! in the moment, then sweeping it under the rug is a solution.

You're at a meeting and don't want your boss to know you are upset. You are a nurse and want to stay strong for your patients. Your partner just upset you with something they said while you were standing with a group of people, and you don't want others to see you react. It could be one of an endless list of reasons.

Sweeping it under the rug gives the appearance that you are unaffected and strong. You get to feel like you have control over your emotions.

Here are some of the other common reasons people have:
- It's not a big deal.
- I don't have time or energy for this now.
- It's easier to just forget about it.
- I'll figure out how to fix this later.
- I don't want to cause a problem.
- What would people think if they knew I felt this way?
- I shouldn't feel this way, so I won't.

It can feel good at that precise moment, as it can feel like you are keeping the peace or rising above it.

Why It's Not

It is hard to go back and look at our Hot Potato after the fact. It hurts. Why re-experience the hurt when it's easier to just move forward? The deeper we bury it, the harder it becomes to deal with later. And each Hot Potato we keep hold of disconnects us from ourselves and our relationships.

While we sweep the Hot Potato under the rug, we are primarily not in connection with ourselves. We don't have compassion for our own hurt. It's like a parent whose child fell off their bike and skinned their knee saying, "Stop crying, that doesn't really hurt so much. You're being a baby! Go play, and we'll take a look at it tomorrow." That's what we do to ourselves.

Sweeping it under the rug can also cause lasting physical pain: *Healing Back Pain—The Mind-Body Connection,* by John E. Sarno is a great example of this in action.

Observation Break

Think of a few times when you have swept something under the rug, where you have ignored (or tried to ignore) a Hot Potato, big or small. Using just a short sentence, write it down with no specific details, and be as factual as possible.

I swept Hot Potato under the rug when (NAME) did / didn't_____.

Some examples might be:

I swept a Hot Potato under the rug . . .

■ . . . when Bob didn't call me on Sunday.

- ... when Alex said I was "incompetent."
- ... when my husband didn't look up from his cell phone.
- ... when my son didn't wash the dishes when I asked him to.
- ... when I lost my keys.

When you think about it, does it affect your body? Do you feel tension somewhere, either mentally, or manifesting as physical pain such as a headache or persistent neck pain?

What are your favorite reasons for ignoring Hot Potatoes?

How often do you do this?

What about other people—when have you seen others that you care about sweep a Hot Potato under the rug?

What reason do they use?

Does this annoy you?

Do you wish they would deal with pain in a different way?

Future Observations

Over the next several days, bring your awareness to the times you sweep things under the rug. Don't change anything; just become aware.

6

BLAME

Another favorite way to handle a Hot Potato is to throw it back at the person you think gave it to you or was an accomplice.

"Take this!!! How could you have done that?" We take our tension and energy and direct it at another person, in the form of blame or criticism. It can be loud and vocal, or it can be stealthily hidden, expressed only in your mind. Either way, it's still blame.

For the longest time, I thought I didn't do that. There is a cute cartoon video online (and at the Online Resources) of a Brené Brown talk on blame. It goes something like this:

One morning, Brené gets up and makes a cup of coffee. Later, she makes a second cup. As she lifts the cup, she accidentally drops it on the floor. It shatters, and she gets coffee all over her white pants. Her first thought was, "Damn you, Steve."

Steve is her husband, and the night before, he arrived home late. He said he'd be home by 10 pm and he knew Brené couldn't fall asleep unless he's in bed with her. Because he returned home late, she didn't fall asleep until later than usual.

The following morning she was tired, so she needed two cups of coffee instead of her usual one. Because it was the second cup that got her pants dirty, in her mind, it was all Steve's fault.

It wasn't like she went through a long, logical thought exercise. As soon as the cup dropped and the coffee splashed onto her pants, she thought, "Damn you, Steve!" That isn't an OUCH!

As I listened to her tell the story, I thought, "Wow, what a bitch! How immature. I would never do that! I would never ever get angry and blame someone else for my own mess up." A week or so later, a moment of self-discovery hit me like a freight train.

Soon after watching the video, I was speaking with Phuc Duong, the Program Manager of the non-profit organization I co-founded in Vietnam. It turns out he was also reading Brené Brown's book, *Daring Greatly*, which had been translated into Vietnamese. We eagerly talked about the book and about the video, and how "other people" always blamed others and how wrong it was. We even gloated about how we never do that. We were in denial.

Every nine months, I traveled around Vietnam with Phuc. We'd been taking these trips annually for years, visiting potential students for our non-profit program in their homes and orphanages, and we'd stay in local hotels along the way. It's important to note, as a foreigner in Vietnam, you can't check into a hotel without a passport.

The weekend after our conversation about Brené Brown, we began our next set of touring and interviews. We arrived at the first hotel and approached the reception desk. The man behind the counter politely asked, "May I have your passport?" Upon hearing his request, my first thought was something like, "Damn you, Phuc!"

I had been checking into hotels in Vietnam for years. I knew the drill. But on this particular occasion, I'd left my passport behind. And my very first thought was, "Damn you, Phuc!"

I wasn't even aware of it. It was immediate, this instantaneous little thought, "Damn you, Phuc! Why didn't you remind me? Damn you, Phuc. You know I'm forgetful. Why didn't you tell me? Damn you, Phuc!"

I was throwing him the Hot Potato, even if only in my head. With my newfound clarity, instead of being upset at myself, I thought, "This is so awesome." I had to share it immediately—"Phuc, Phuc, remember that thing I said NEVER happens to me? I do it. I am simply not aware of it."

Tension is not fun. It's a frigging Hot Potato!!! If you don't want a Hot Potato in your hand (or your head), why not simply give it to somebody else? Giving it to another person is deflecting. It's like pushing the responsibility for the pain towards someone else.

As a surprise, Phuc went and got *Damn You, Phuc* t-shirts made for everyone. He got a *Damn You, Phuc* t-shirt for his wife and another one for his little daughter. I have a collection of *Damn You, Phuc* t-shirts that I sporadically give to friends.

Blaming, being right, being defensive, they all fit into this category. And it happens all the time, ALLLLL the time.

Now you also might be thinking, "But I never *say* anything, I only *think it*." Watch your thoughts. Maybe you are the same as me, not even aware of what you're thinking. I want to challenge you, the next time you get a Hot Potato, what are you thinking?

I had this experience in India, where a teacher spoke to us about anger. I was in a headspace where my thoughts were slowed down enough for me to see what I thought about a former partner. I knew all the things "they" said about me because it was so loud, but what I hadn't examined were my internal words.

The teacher instructed us to review the conversations we were having in our heads with a specific person. I concentrated intensely, and soon I could see and hear them clearly. There actually were conversations, things I wanted to say to him but never did. I thought about all the blame I shifted onto him and all the harsh words I used in my head. It was so much worse than anything he'd ever said to me. My defense had always been, "Yeah, but I never said them out loud." But the reality was, even in just thinking it, I was no different from him.

You might have noticed, the incident with my former husband forgetting his passport with me so many years ago is not so very different from me forgetting my passport with Phuc. With my new awareness of how easy it was to handle a Hot Potato this way, I could totally forgive my former husband. In fact, the awareness made it so there wasn't even anything to forgive.

Why It's Awesome

Anger and blame create a wonderful rush of chemicals that make us feel strong and powerful. It doesn't just make us *feel* stronger; it truly *makes* us stronger. When we are angry, Adrenaline and other hormones are released, thereby increasing your physical strength and your resistance to pain.

You might need or want this energy to do something. And, as with all these Hot Potatoes handlings, there is a time you might choose to use it.

Why It's Not

In relationships, blame creates disconnection and defensive-ness.

It might feel like we are solving the problem, but in many ways, we are simply creating more. Even when we change a relationship—say in a divorce or dissolving a business partnership—the energy used to blame is immense. Anger and the subsequent hormones released with the fight response are not meant to last. They are meant to give us a short, extra boost to vanquish our enemies.

If we keep going back to this moment over and over again, or hold onto it, it overdrives our body, causing lowered immune systems, high blood pressure, or heart disease.

It can feel great in the moment, but afterward, we can feel guilty for saying or doing what we did, either getting angrier or adding another type of Hot Potato handling to the mix.

While we are experiencing anger and blame towards someone, it is impossible to connect. We are no longer on the same side of the table with them. They are the enemy. And it is quite possible that this attack creates a Hot Potato for them, and so they throw it back at YOU.

Observation Break

Think of times when you blamed someone—threw a Hot Potato at them—either secretly or openly? Write these down using just a short sentence, with no details, and be as factual as possible. Write out or say aloud what you did with your Hot Potato and whether it was secret or in the open.

Some examples might be:

- I openly threw a Hot Potato at Pete when he broke my computer.
- I secretly threw a Hot Potato at my mother when she criticized my plans.
- I openly threw a Hot Potato at Esther when she didn't keep something confidential.
- I secretly threw a Hot Potato at my boss when she didn't promote me.
- I openly threw a Hot Potato at my daughter when she failed her French class.

What did you do or say or simply think?

Who did you say this to?

Did it make you feel stronger, more righteous?

What is your go-to reasoning when you throw a Hot Potato? Here are some of the more common thoughts people get:

- They deserve it. It's their fault.
- If they hadn't said that, I wouldn't have been hurt.
- How could they do that?
- Only an idiot would do that.
- I hate them.
- I need to punish them so they will never do that again.

Are there others that you would like to add to the list?

Which one is your favorite?

How often do you think this?

Really take a look, even though looking at tension isn't easy. That's why we've created so many clever ways to deal with it.

Future Observations

Over the next several days, bring your awareness to the times you blame, (in your head or out loud), and to the person who hurt you or to someone else. Don't change anything; just become aware.

7

SELF-BLAME

Self-blame is in the same category as blame. Life hands you a Hot Potato. Perhaps there's an accident or a mistake. Something painful happens, and you feel like there is no one to blame but yourself. You don't fully feel the OUCH! and therefore, you don't say it.

All sorts of things happen in life. Often, when the unimaginable happens, it is better to blame ourselves than to feel out of control. For me, it was with my father's death. He had chronic pain in his stomach, but waited months to have it checked out. When he was in the hospital for exploratory surgery, he died. The self-blame I experienced was overwhelming. Why didn't I convince him to see someone earlier? Why didn't I get to him sooner so I could have been there during the operation? Why didn't I stay living in Michigan so I could take care of him? It went on and on and on.

It doesn't have to only be "big" things. It can be something small, but it still packs the same punch. Finishing a project late, forgetting to call a friend on their birthday, or perhaps breaking a very expensive champagne glass that someone gave you for a wedding gift.

Your immediate reaction may be feeling like you need to punish yourself so you don't EVER do that again. Unlike blame, where you are the accuser and have been harmed, in self-blame, you are both the accuser and the accused.

The harder you blame (which makes you feel more in control), the more you hurt, which makes you feel less in control. It is dangerous because you can't really disconnect from yourself.

Another part of self-blame is thinking, "If I were a better person, partner, employee, this wouldn't have happened." This inevitably leads to another thought: "I need to be better; I'm not good enough." So, the action becomes focused on becoming better.

Not for the joy of it, but to make sure you are never upset again.

For example, let's say after the first time you failed an exam (maybe you didn't, but I did, receiving an F in Japanese), you never released your OUCH!, and instead held onto it so you could remember to be more perfect and prevent this Hot Potato from happening to you again. However, to know what was "wrong" with you, and what needed to be perfected, you must constantly focus on the Hot Potato and hold onto it. And it goes round and round and round. Such intense focus can create a life of excellence and striving, but also one of intense tension and self-judgment.

It can cause us to cover up parts of ourselves we think are imperfect. We stuff these "imperfections" into a drawer along with the hurt, in the same way that I throw clutter into a closet when unexpected guests show up.

Just to clarify, self-guidance and self-blame are two completely different things. It is pretty easy to tell the difference. Let's say that your teenage son started yelling at you in public and stormed out of the restaurant during dinner. Self-blame might sound like, "How could I have raised such a son? I'm a failure as a mother." Guidance might sound like "I might want to use a different way of connecting with him when he gets angry like that."

Self-blame is about judging and labeling yourself for something that happened in the past.

Self-guidance is about using the experience to allow you to create a better future.

Why It's Awesome

You feel you will be able to absorb all the "heat" of the Hot Potato, by placing all the responsibility squarely on your shoulders.

It can act as a deterrent to doing the same thing again. It can be a motivator. It starts you making amends. And it's possible that it can shift away from the energy of blame and regret and morph into an effortless look at possibilities to be and behave differently.

Why It's Not

You can't run away from yourself—the best you can do to stop the cycle of self-blame (other than dissolving the hurt tied up with it) is to cut off parts of yourself. Self-blame can keep us from being ourselves and from being free to simply be. Everywhere you self-blame is a place you are rejecting yourself. It can create a compulsion of wanting someone else to love all of you when you don't even accept all parts of yourself.

Observation Break

Can you think of times when you've blamed yourself?

Write them down. Just notice, don't add self-judgment to self-blame.

Examples:

- I blamed myself for not being sexy enough when my husband left me.
- I blamed myself for not being disciplined with my eating when a friend said that I was overweight.
- I blamed myself for being insensitive when I hurt my friend's feelings.
- I blamed myself for being clumsy when I spilled coffee on Sarah's dress.

- I blamed myself for being unlovable when my boyfriend chose to have Christmas with his family instead of me.

What were the good reasons for blaming yourself? Can you experiment with blaming yourself even more? How does that feel?

What is your go-to reasoning when you self-blame and feel like you are not good enough? Here are some of the more common thoughts people get:

- I deserve it.
- I need to figure out what is wrong with me so that never happens again.
- I can never forgive myself.
- I need to face the truth.
- If it's my fault, I'll be able to fix it.

Which is your favorite? How often do you do this? Really take a look. Looking at tension isn't easy. This is why we've created so many clever ways to deal with it.

Bring your awareness to the times you have self-blamed. Just notice, ask yourself, what were you wanting to accomplish, and how were you wanting to feel?

It can feel like there is at least someone who caused the hurt, YOU. How can you have a loving relationship with someone else when you don't even want to have a relationship with yourself?

8

RUN

Sometimes we catch a Hot Potato while we are in a specific place or situation, such as a job, in a relationship, in a town, etc. We figure, if we can just move to a new spot, the Hot Potatoes won't follow us there. So, we pack up and move.

In the romantic relationships in my life as I wrote earlier, I was like Goldilocks. Each relationship lasted 8–10 years. If I had to summarize where I felt the hurt was coming from at the time, it was probably something like this:

The relationship in my 20s: I wasn't seen, I wasn't heard, and he didn't communicate. I spent countless nights crying myself to sleep, feeling all alone. Eventually, I left him. I just told him one day that it was over, and left the same night, moving to a different part of town.

My 30s: I was watched closely, but only for my flaws, it seemed! I felt like I was walking on eggshells, and I never knew what was going to set him off. If you've seen the film *Sleeping with the Enemy*, the image for me was a scene where Julia Roberts is soooooo careful about how she arranged the towels in the bathroom. I felt alone and afraid all the time. So, I left him and moved to another city.

My 40s: All of the above, plus a deep sense of inadequacy. Alone, afraid, confused, and living in a foreign country. I remember—with my deepest apologies to women who have been physically abused—wishing I had visible bruises. It didn't seem fair to me that I had to carry all that hurt inside where no one could see it. So, I left him and moved to another country.

Part of turning everything around in my life was my figuring out that, after three men (who were all very different from one another) kept hurting me so deeply, it was probably something about me, not them.

You might say good riddance to those guys. Years later, after releasing the pain, I can now look back at each one with fondness. There is now more ease, more connection, and more acceptance.

Some people run after the first Hot Potato, some after the 1,000th.

Running isn't about changing your life, which often makes sense. Instead, it's the idea that by running from a place or relationship, you will stop your hurt and never be hurt again.

Running happens everywhere. I just had trouble with my iPhone after a car ran over it. Another unsaid OUCH! While trying to get it repaired, I was getting frustrated with Apple Technical Support telling me I couldn't get it repaired in Puerto Rico, nor could I do a mail-in repair from Puerto Rico. After I hung up to wait for someone from a different department to call me, my first thought was, "I'm going to switch to an Android!" Can you see it? Even before I got a resolution, I was already mentally running to the competitor. I noticed my thought and just had to laugh.

Let me again say, I don't recommend staying in a group or relationship that isn't ultimately supporting where you are going with your life. But if you dissolve the tension before making a change, you won't compulsively run into the same situation over and over again, merely with different people in different places.

Why It's Awesome

Running can feel sooooo freeing. I remember after my divorce, I felt so liberated, so alive. I could do whatever I wanted, whenever I wanted, with whomever I wanted. When you run, you can be yourself and start over creating the life you want.

Sometimes running is crucial to your actual physical safety! You can get away from harm.

It can also give you the distance from the situation to reflect, without all the tension.

When I say these handlings are awesome, I mean it. There are times and places for each of these.

Why It's Not

Running creates disconnection with the person you are in a relationship with. There are actually ways to change the character of a relationship without running. Gwyneth Paltrow popularized the term "conscious uncoupling." Friends of mine divorced, they had a joint divorce party to celebrate their marriage and their family.

Running can create endless seeking for the ONE: for the ONE right person, the ONE right job, the ONE right friend, the ONE right house . . . the ONE right cell phone company.

Without internal observation, it can create a never-ending search, where you never feel at home. It is impossible to be connected if you aren't there physically or emotionally.

Observation Break

Can you think of times when you ran from a relationship, a job, or a friend? Either emotionally (still together, but disconnected, or cutting ties or time with them). Write it out or say it out loud with what you did with your Hot Potato and your reason.

Here are some examples:

- I emotionally ran from my mother, going to live with my dad, when I felt she was ignoring me.
- I ran from my boyfriend, leaving the house and running to the woods when he broke a plate in anger.
- I ran from my job, by quitting and finding another job

when they took my corner office away.

- I emotionally ran from Kasey, by not being as friendly to her at the staff party, after she called attention to a mistake I'd made in front of everyone.

Did you feel free?
What is your go-to reasoning when you run?

Here are some of the more common thoughts people have:

- I can find someone/something better.
- In my next relationship, I'll never feel this way.
- I'm sure the next one will be better.
- They don't deserve me.

What is your favorite? How often do you do this? Really take a look. Looking at tension isn't easy. That's why we've created so many clever ways to deal with it.

It can feel like being able to live again, to have hope. But we can end up with the same feelings in the next relationship, and what happens when there is nowhere else to run?

Bring your awareness to the times you have run. Don't judge or defend; just notice them and ask yourself, what were you looking for, how were you wanting to feel without that relationship? Did you want more connection, more understanding, more love?

9

HIDE

Hiding is the sister to running; it's similar, and yet it's different. When you are running, you are running to another possibility. With hiding, there is really no place to run. With running, there is the hope of something better. With hiding, there is a fear of something worse.

It is not wanting to ever come out and play in some area of life, relationships, community, jobs, or friends. One example of this is with a cat I once had. If he was scared by some noise or sudden movement, he would jump and immediately run to the other side of the room.

When I first brought him to my home, he had been on a plane from San Francisco for six hours, and then in a car for another two. He'd been taken away from his mother, his brothers and sisters, and the only home he'd ever known. To him, everything was dangerous. When I let him out of his carrier, he hid in a bedroom and stayed there for days. I worried he wouldn't come out and eat.

It is easy to think, of course, he is a cat; that's normal behavior when they are scared. It is also 'normal' for people.

I hid. I hid a lot. I remember doing this after one difficult experience with my partner. I don't remember what set it off, or what set him off. I don't recall any of the details. What I do remember is feeling so alone and so hurt, just wanting to escape, but having nowhere to go. I locked myself in the guest room for almost two days. I cried and I slept, then cried some more. I snuck out only to use the bathroom and get a glass of water. I didn't pick up the phone. I didn't even eat.

I eventually came out, but it was a pattern that repeated itself again and again. Not so different from the times when I was five years old and hid under my bed when I was upset with my mother.

Habits build up over time. On the chronic side, as relates to romantic relationships, it can look like someone not even trying to have relationships, even if they really do want them. Being alone doesn't have to be physically hiding; it can be simply hiding your heart.

The thoughts might be that "relationships are too hard," or "I'm not good enough," or "men are all worthless," or "women are crazy." It can be things like, "I don't ever want to connect to my partner again, cause I'll be hurt," or "I keep getting hurt," or "I don't want (INSERT YOUR OWN EXAMPLE), so I won't try again."

It is the idea of not ever wanting to go there again because it will be too painful. It is building walls and hiding from the Hot Potatoes, locking yourself in a room, and not wanting to go out. If my five-year-old self had stayed under my bed forever, what would my life be like? If my forty-three-year-old self had stayed permanently locked in a room, what would my life be like? Maybe safe, but also very, very, very lonely. How long have you hidden?

Why It's Awesome

You are safe! It's a place to recover and heal. There is the possibility of time to reflect.

There is absolutely nothing wrong with hiding. It is normal, especially for cats after cross-continental journeys.

And in physical situations of danger, hiding can be lifesaving. I'm all for hiding out from imminent physical threat.

Why It's Not

You are alone. If you keep doing this, or if this becomes a habit, you will stay alone.

Being alone and the feeling of loneliness is (as mentioned earlier) more dangerous to your health than smoking fifteen cigarettes a day.

Observation Break

Recall some times in your past when you hid.

Examples:

- I physically hid from my family during holidays, staying at home alone, when everyone got into an argument the year before.
- I emotionally hid, never wanting to be vulnerable to hurt again after my wife left me.
- I emotionally hid from groups of women after a friend embarrassed me in front of others.
- I emotionally and physically hid from men I might date after too many guys "ghosted" me.

There are lots of good reasons for doing this. What were yours?

How long did you hide?

Are there currently areas of your life where you are hiding?

What is your go-to reasoning when hiding? Here are some of the more common thoughts people get:

- I don't want to go through that again.
- I need a break.
- I'm better off alone.
- I'm too tired.
- I just need to rest.
- People are too difficult. I prefer pets.

Which is your favorite? How often do you do this?

It can feel like no place is safe. However, if you are hiding, just like running, you will never experience the connection you want (which I'm assuming you do, since you are investing the time in reading this book).

Bring your awareness to the major times in your life when you have hidden. Look at the judgments about yourself or the "outside," (we have ALL done it). Just notice and ask yourself, "What if I felt safe? How much would I be willing to love."

10

REASONS & RULES

Reasons and rules are one of the most prevalent ways we try to stop getting hurt. It's not just in romantic relationships; it's also with children, friends, neighbors, and strangers. So, let's start with the "Oh shit!" guy.

Once, in the middle of one of my workshops, a man blurted out, "Oh shit!" Wondering what was going on, I stopped. "You just dropped an anvil of truth on me!" he exclaimed. He went on to explain how he used this method to protect himself from the sickening feeling of hearing "no" from potential clients. He signed up for every workshop, read every book, and went on an exhausting quest to find the right selling rules, all for the purpose of not getting rejected.

Humans are amazing at figuring things out, seeing how things work, taking them apart and putting them back together again, and we are particularly good at making nature bend to our will. If you step back and look at the world, look at what we have built—from massive cities to tiny electronics, and our field of vision from the Hubble Space Telescope to subatomic particles—it is almost unbelievable. Yes, I know, we have also

caused mass extinctions, perhaps irreparable damage to the atmosphere, and depleted the earth of its stored-up sunlight, but look at what we have created.

We wouldn't have been able to do this without our beautiful

ability to dissect, label, and mold things, and then pass that knowledge on with language and learning, sharing reasons and rules about the world.

Where we get in trouble is in looking at our relationships and the people in them as objects.

I would never have wanted to live in our apartment in NYC—which was built in 1930 and stands 1,000 ft over Manhattan—if there weren't exact measurements, exact specifications, and exact blueprints. There are whole industries built around creating standards and doing quality control on material objects. It is amazing. The ability we have to build and plan is truly staggering.

But again, people aren't objects.

Everywhere we look, it seems like we're being told that there is a formula (rules). Here were some top hits from Google when I just searched about relationships:

- Four techniques to make anyone fall in love with you.
- How to use psychology to make someone fall (and stay) in love with you.
- Five ways to make a woman want to have sex with you.
- How to make your child a math genius.

One of the clearest ways to look at this is from being on the receiving end. How would you feel if someone was searching for rules to get you to behave differently? It just doesn't feel right, it isn't loving, and it isn't connecting.

Reasons always lead us back to "because." We do all this research to learn about others so that we have reasons why things happened.

- "He hurt my feelings because he has a low emotional IQ."
- "I don't want to get close to anyone because of my divorce."

- "I am defensive because my mother was controlling."
- "We don't have a good relationship because we don't communicate."

Although this may make us feel better and feel that we are in control, it doesn't necessarily help heal the hurt. It makes us feel like we understand it. But as we will learn later, it can invariably create more hurt in the future.

There is a great story that explains this in further detail. It explains the "reason" you get coffee on your clothes when someone bumps into you.

You are walking down a hallway with a cup of coffee, when someone accidentally bumps into you, spilling hot coffee everywhere.

Why did you spill the coffee?

"Because someone bumped into me!!!"

Wrong answer.

You spilled the hot coffee because there was coffee in your cup.

Had there been hot tea in the cup, you would have spilled hot tea.

Whatever is inside the cup is what will spill out.

Therefore, when life comes along and shakes you (which WILL happen), whatever is inside you will come out. It's easy to fake it until you get rattled.

So, we must ask ourselves . . . "What's in my cup?"

When life gets tough, what spills over? Joy, gratefulness, peace, and humility? Or anger, bitterness, harsh words, and reactions?

Life provides the cup, but YOU choose how to fill it.

It's an awesome story and a great analogy about your inner state. In some ways, though, you could also say the reason the hot coffee spilled on you is because you were in the hallway at that time. You could say it was because you couldn't get to the office you were going to without walking down the hallway, and you could say it is because you are right-handed (If you were left-handed, the coffee would have been in the other hand). You could say it is because of gravity or the qualities of liquid in the cup. The list is endless.

None of this helps, nor matters when it comes to the topic of this book. The friggin' coffee is hot! It hurts! OUCH! Finding the reason doesn't support healing the pain.

We like to arbitrarily choose one thing and grab onto it as "The Reason" when in truth, the number of actual causes is infinite.

Why It's Awesome

We have incredible minds; why not use them? Most of the time, we can figure out a strategy to change our environment.

We try to use it to change people who are not objects. And while there seems to be always a cause and effect. There are innumerable reasons going into why each event occurs.

Why It's Not

Creating a complex (or simple) list of rules to never get hurt again does not release the initial hurt. In fact, we often hold onto a Hot Potato in order to keep investigating it or trying to understand it.

Observation Break

Recall something that is still hurting you.

Do you have a specific reason why it happened? If so, try this:

How many other reasons are there that could have caused that to happen?

Has anyone tried to enforce their rules on you? If so, what were they?

What rules have you enforced on others?

11

NUMB & DISTRACT

It might be said that everything we do that keeps us from dissolving a Hot Potato is an effort to numb or distract. But most distractions are usually pleasurable things that help take our minds off the pain.

Let me give you an example. A man I was dating said he would see me on Saturday. On Friday, though, when he called, he made no mention of our plans. Instead, he told me that he was going out with friends the next night. OUCH!

Even though it hurt, I didn't say OUCH! because I was determined not to be needy. I decided to go for a walk to "get over it." I closed my laptop, headed out the door, turned right . . . and spotted one of my favorite Irish pubs. Sure, it was only 4pm, but I thought to myself, "*I deserve a pint of Guinness.*" Thankfully, this occurred at a time after I had started to become aware of all the ways I was escaping the hurt . . . so I kept walking.

As I turned the corner, there was a pâtisserie that sold my favorite raspberry macarons. "*I deserve a macaron!*" I thought. I stopped and acknowledged the thought, then kept going.

Around the next turn was a pop-up sample sale. "*Yay!! Clothes!!!*" I noticed that this thought felt exactly the same as wanting the Guinness and the macaron. It was a way to feel better, to soothe myself with some external treat. I'll admit it, I walked into the store, looked around, and spotted a new coat, but didn't buy it. The feeling of shopping and the words in my head were the same: "*I deserve it.*"

The "I deserve it" distraction isn't the only one. We can distract ourselves in so many ways, even with activities that are helpful, such as work, exercise, and even self-improvement, and meditation. It isn't so much what we do; it is the urge, (perhaps unconscious), behind it.

I've had clients who are so successful in business. They work constantly, run large companies, are loved by their staff, and yet are miserable at home. Work distracts them from their unhappiness with their family.

It can even be true with meditation, self-improvement, or sports. It can sound like, "Well, if I can't have a happy marriage, at least I can finish that triathlon" or "I hate my husband, but I'll learn to love the universe."

Again, it's not that either isn't a perfectly healthy activity, but what is the motivation? Something as simple as going to see a movie on a date can be motivated by wanting to share an experience *or* trying to avoid connection.

Honestly, we numb and distract ourselves from hurt all the time. Sometimes, it is simply about choosing the best way to numb or distract in the moment.

An example from my teen years looked (from the outside), like dedication and commitment. As a teenager, I had had a very difficult relationship with my mother and her new husband, Bob. I couldn't stand being in the room with him, and I couldn't even talk about my mom to others beyond a surface level without breaking into tears. When she remarried, I felt both abandoned and like a barrier to her happiness. Bad combination! The summer I was home from college, I didn't want to be with them, AT ALL. So, I took up long-distance running.

Every night after work, I would run ten miles. When I got home after running, I would sleep till noon, get up and go to work, and then start all over again. Everyone was so impressed with how dedicated I was. They marveled at how toned my legs had become. But I spent the whole summer there and I don't think I ate one meal with my mom and new stepfather.

Now, as it turns out, Bob is a seriously great guy. In my 40s, we finally became friends, and he was my go-to person for so many of life's questions. Having looked at this with new eyes, I can see how it would have been better to have simply numbed myself a bit with some red wine and joined them for dinner or a TV show. That way, there was at least a hope of connection. Instead, I wasted twenty years not having a close relationship with him or my mother.

Numbing and distracting, at its essence, is turning your attention and life energy not *towards* something you are passionate about, but *away* from something you are avoiding.

Your body and mind might be doing all sorts of things, but you are living in a pile of Hot Potatoes and doing everything you can to not notice them.

Why It's Awesome

You get a mental break, a vacation. You get to do something that feels better than what you were feeling. Drug highs, exercise highs, meditation highs, volunteering—they can all feel amazing. It feels so much better than the pain.

Why It's Not

It reduces your awareness, and the Hot Potato becomes less visible. You stop doing things because you are truly passionate about them—because they are an outlet for your creativity and joy—and instead, you do them solely to escape. You can forget what real joy feels like.

Observation Break

How many different ways do you numb and distract?

There are so, so many, but I'll just list a few. Remember to only examine the ones that have the motivation of avoiding the pain with some pleasure.

- Drinking
- Drugs
- Working
- Eating
- Exercising
- Self-Improvement
- Volunteering
- Hobbies
- Social Media
- Video Games
- Sports
- The News
- Sex
- Shopping

Can you think of more?
Which ones are your favorites?
Do they differ for different people or situations?
How do these distractions or numbing alternatives make you feel?
Are there any that have become habits?

What is your go-to reasoning when numbing and distracting?

Here are some of the more common thoughts people get:

- I deserve to _____.
- At least I can be happy when I am _____.
- _____ will make me happy.
- I could at least _____.

Which is your favorite? How often do you do this?

It can feel like some pleasure is better than dealing with all that hurt, and it is. However, if you are numbing and distracting to the point where it becomes a full-time habit, you'll deny yourself the rich experience of a joy-filled life.

Bring your awareness to the times you have numbed or distracted. This is one question where you have to be completely honest with yourself—does it feel deeply fulfilling, or is it more like an escape?

12

DAYDREAM & HOPE

Daydreaming is similar to numbing and distracting and maybe a bit like running too, except that you are mentally running into the future. It can sound in your head like "When I ____" or "If only I ____" Fill in your own blanks.

I want to touch on the idea of Being vs. Doing.

"Being" is the state you are in. It could be a beautiful state such as love, connection, joy, intimacy, or authenticity. It could be a suffering state, such as disconnection, hurt, inadequacy, or scarcity.

"Doing" is what you accomplish in life, and visualizing goals is an important part of it. No building would ever be built without someone first seeing it in their mind and then sketching the rough plans based on their mental vision.

Daydreaming is something different, as it relates to Hot Potatoes. It is more like someone thinking, "When I have a life partner, I'll feel complete," or, "When I'm successful, I'll be confident." It could also be saying things like, "When I can finally pay my bills, I won't be so anxious," or, "After I have children, I can finally

relax," or, on the flip side, "After my children have left home, I can finally relax."

Beneath all these thoughts is a Hot Potato (or maybe a lot of them) that these daydreamers and hopers want to STOP experiencing.

Every time someone daydreams like this, for a moment, an hour, a day, or sometimes even years, it is building up the idea that for a hurt to go away, something external must happen. Or in order to have joy, an external event has to occur.

I want you to look at something, and it's something I know

THE POWER OF OUCH!

in every cell of my body to be true. *Being is independent of achieving.* The idea that you have to have achieved a level of financial success, or a certain weight, or be married or with a partner, or own a certain car, or live in a certain neighborhood, or have some political party in office, or be younger or be older (I could go on and on) . . . NONE of those is a prerequisite to being in a beautiful (Hot Potato-less) state.

If this seems way too far-fetched of an idea, you might want to take some time out and read *Chasing Daylight—How My Forthcoming Death Transformed My Life,* by Eugene O'Kelley, or *Man's Search for Meaning,* by Viktor E. Frankl. Reading first-hand accounts of joy or fulfillment found despite a diagnosis of an incurable and inoperable brain tumor, or living in a Nazi concentration camp, can turn your view of life on its head.

Realize that joy, authentic connection, or a beautiful experience are all things that are available to you right now. Holding onto hurt from the past is not solved by imagining a future where all the conditions are perfect for you to be in a state of love, joy, connection, peace, confidence, compassion, relaxation, or whatever it is you desire.

My father dreamed of buying a sailboat and living on it, sailing from our home in Michigan to Florida in the winters. He loved the idea of that boat, and he lived for the idea of it, constantly reading boating magazines and visiting friends on their boats. Boat-obsessed, as you can see!

I also remember how disconnected he and my mom were in their marriage, and I vividly remember him hating his job, his boss, the hours he worked, and the constant stress he was under. He was also a distant father as I was growing up, and we were never close.

In my forties, we reconnected, and I got a chance to know him better. I also got to see his dream become a reality.

After thirty-one years, he finally bought his boat—a fifty-six-foot Hans Christian. It was beautiful. I flew up to Michigan to spend two weeks on it with him. What an amazing trip it was!! Getting to be with my dad as he started to live his long-awaited dream, was in itself, a dream come true. We had so many adventures during our trip, including fog, freighters, friends, and family. It was a celebration of his new life.

In October, he put the boat away for winter storage and to varnish the decks and paint the hull for his upcoming voyages. In December, he died.

As happy as the boat made him (and me) on our trip, I was never sure that those two weeks balanced out all the prior stress. I've told this story to others, who have said, "Well, at least he got to experience it with you." And that is so true. Others have said, "But he got to enjoy the thirty-one years planning for it." Again, very true.

He enjoyed the moments when he could do something towards acquiring the boat, but the rest of the time, it seemed to me as though he suffered in the present.

It was the opinion of some close to him that the stomach condition leading to the hospital stay was caused by his thirty-one years of stress. Maybe, maybe not. I don't know. However, as a lesson on how to live one's life, I look at this as a reminder not to postpone joy.

Why It's Awesome

Dreaming is amazing. Our ability to create wonderful futures in our minds is almost miraculous.

Just like numbing and distracting, it can create relief. It's a vacation we can take in our minds.

Why It's Not

Also, like numbing and distracting, done over and over, it creates a habit that is hard to break.

Living in the future, no matter how beautiful that future may be, leaves little room to connect with the present. Other people are only in the present. Relationships are only in the present. Life is in the present—not the past, not the future.

Observation Break

What do you daydream about?

Which emotions do you experience when you believe your daydream will come true?

What is your go-to reasoning when daydreaming? Here are some of the more common thoughts people get:

- Someday, when _____, then it will be alright.
- I can't wait until _____, so I can be happy.
- If only _____ would happen.
- I may be miserable now, but in the future, I will ____?

Which is your favorite, and how often do you do this?

None of this is to say that plans, dreams, and desires aren't absolutely vital. The thing to watch out for is whether you are using this to wait to be connected or joyful?

Bring your awareness to your images of the future. What did you do in the last week to move towards that image? Have you done anything about reaching this future or just imagined it? If you imagine never achieving that future, what thoughts pop up?

13

OFFERINGS & SACRIFICES

Since ancient times, humans have had the idea that if you gave offerings to the gods, they would protect you from harm and hurt. In the past, this was as extreme as human sacrifice or as innocuous as lighting a candle in a temple.

In relationships, it could be a spouse buying a gift to stop the argument. It is a child coming home for the holidays, when he would prefer to be with friends, just to prevent his parents from haranguing him.

How is this related to saying OUCH!? How is this holding onto the hurt? It's easy to think that hurt can be stopped or prevented by giving in or giving offerings, but in fact, it holds the hurt in place. "I'll just do even more than I do so that they won't hurt me," is one example. Another is, "I need to be better to make up for my faults." This was me, and I guess that's why I mentioned gifts in the example above. I would go to extremes thinking of the perfect gift, not because I was a happy gift-giver—as many people I know are (gifts are not my love language)—but to try to stave off hurt.

I had the idea that if I could give a better present or throw a bigger party, they wouldn't hurt my feelings again. This went to the extreme of a full-on dance troupe with traditional music and taking over a whole restaurant for a private dinner and show. It wasn't for the joy of it; it was with the thought that "Maybe this will do the trick. Maybe it will make him treat me better, so I can feel loved."

It can become a form of sacrifice, where you start to resent what you are doing, considering it to be a burden. Plus, the more you sacrifice, the more you feel you are owed in return.

This Hot Potato can be followed by thoughts that starts with, "After everything I've done for you . . . " Examples of this might be:

- After everything I've sacrificed for you, at least you could be on time.
- After everything I've given you, you still don't treat me with respect.
- After everything I do for you, why can't you pay attention to me rather than your phone?

The many ways we handle Hot Potatoes are really attempts to avoid being hurt again. Offerings and sacrifices are all based on commerce . . . if I give you this, then you should give me that. Commerce works on Amazon, but not necessarily with loving relationships and authentic connection.

Why It's Awesome

It feels like we are doing something proactive and loving. What could be wrong with buying gifts or sacrificing for another? There is a certain amount of pride that comes with this and a sense of having contributed.

Why It's Not

We think we are not good enough, or we are not doing enough.

We sacrifice more and more and end up getting less and less love and connection.

Observation Break

Think of a time when you have done so much for a person, yet they've still hurt you.

What were some of the things you did for them?

How far out of your way are you willing to go to make them happy?

Are there ways you could be better or more perfect to prevent future hurt?

Take it from me; if you are creating a relationship based on sacrifice, no matter what you do and what you give, it will never work.

14

FILE

Filing is similar to the Sweep It Under the Rug chapter. However, the intent isn't to hide it, but simply to file it for later use.

An amazing woman in my life, Gale, describes this beautifully when she told me about a "red flag" in a new romantic relationship.

They were just about to go out, and Gale complimented her girlfriend on how beautiful she looked, expecting a similar compliment back. Instead, the woman replied, "Don't you think you want to do something with your hair?" Yikes! Big OUCH!, but she didn't say it. Later, as other events occurred, she referred to that original Hot Potato.

I know exactly what she was talking about because it happened to me. I would always use the first Hot Potato in my relationship and file it away, just in case other ones might show up, which they inevitably did. Then, later I would always look back to the first incident, saying I "should have known." In fact, because I had collected and filed one Hot Potato, I was always hunting for more!

Plus, I never allowed anyone to know how much a specific moment hurt me. If they had reacted to a genuine OUCH! from me by never going out with me again, yes, I would have hurt for a short time, but I would have saved myself so much more time and pain.

Why It's Awesome

You may want to be strategic and careful by looking for both the "good" and the "bad." Remember though, the tendency is to look for the negatives so make sure to hunt even harder for the "good."

Why It's Not

Each small OUCH! inevitably grows. Not saying OUCH! early on makes it harder to say later. We tend to file a negative OUCH! more than a positive YAY! So, in this mode, even the kindest person can show up with a bunch of Hot Potatoes filed under their name.

Observation Break

What is something that you think might be a Hot Potato, that you are filing?

How long have you held on to it?

How many other Hot Potatoes will you need to collect before you acknowledge there is pain?

What would life be like if you couldn't store up those Hot Potatoes for later use?

The point I want to stress here is that it's a conscious decision to either express the OUCH! there and then, or have to address it further down the road—and inevitably, choosing the latter option is always more tumultuous, painful, negative, exhausting, and hurtful.

15

ENLIST

I spend a lot of time talking face-to-face with people about hurt and relationships. I am part of many groups where this is a frequently discussed topic. There is a common method of dealing with a Hot Potato, especially with women, that goes something like this: "Let me tell you what happened, they did this, then they did that, then that, and that was like this other thing over here." Then they will ask, "What do you think I should do?"

This question unleashes everyone's opinion about how to handle a Hot Potato, be it run, blame, hide, or research. Common responses include:

- "You don't deserve to be hurt."

- "He's an asshole, forget him."

- "What did you do to create that?"

Rarely do you hear a simple "OUCH!"

Think about all the times you have asked or answered the question, "What do you think I should do?" Did the group feel

your pain and react? We take on the pain of another in two ways, not only by mirroring their feelings but also by living their stories. We hear someone speak, and we react as if we were the main character, with all *our* history, not theirs, and then we lobby to have them react the way we would, using our own Hot Potato handling.

No one can ever react or act for us. They can, of course, provide support, advice, and opinions—which, if taken as suggestions only—can be very helpful. What is important though, is to understand what those possibilities are intended for: stopping you from being hurt, or allowing you to be you and experience life and share the beauty of who you really are.

Why It's Awesome

Nothing happens alone. Other people can share their experiences and open up worlds of possibilities, giving us more choices.

Support is also available from friends and family who can just be there and listen without adding all their ideas of how to avoid the pain.

Why It's Not

If we don't ask the right questions, we will get the wrong answers. If we ask the question while holding onto a Hot Potato, it's likely to come out as, "How do I deal with this?" which will simply lead to a different kind of Hot Potato handling, not a dissolution.

A group can greatly influence how you think and act, and in many instances, it's not the right advice for you, because they're not YOU.

Observation Break

Think of a current hurt that has you asking others, "What do you think I should do?"

Who would you say this to?

Do they listen without interjecting, or do they suggest yet another Hot Potato handling?

16

REWINDING & REPLAYING

Rewinding & Replaying can occur in tandem with all the above Hot Potato handlings. We keep rewinding and replaying the event, looking for something we might have missed.

With each replay of the hurtful event, we feel hurt all over again. We continuously trigger ourselves. Nothing has happened in the "real" world. Our thoughts simply create the hurt once more.

When someone hurts you and you replay it over and over and over again, the math goes something like this:

A friend says something hurtful to me. What she says takes her ten seconds to say and ten seconds for me to hear. I play it on repeat in my mind for hours. In doing so, it hurts me so much more. Then, I attribute ALL my newly amassed hurt to her.

You might want to say, "Oh, but she started it." Yes, she said what she said, but I continued it, and continued it, and continued it.

Let's calculate this. She spent ten seconds saying what she said, and I spent hours replaying it. Let's say I spend only an hour

thinking about it and reliving it. That's 10 seconds for something she did and 3,600 seconds for something I did. Then I attribute every single one of those 3,610 seconds to her.

This one, combined with any of the others, is so damaging because it keeps the hurt, pain, and suffering alive.

Why It's Awesome

There are some therapies that rely on reliving the details of the experience over and over to desensitize it. This can help release trauma, negative emotions, and painful experiences. If it is done without the intention to change the past and to simply see the events as they were, it can create a sense of well-being.

I would recommend getting a professional to guide you through this type of therapy, as there is a danger of getting "trapped" in the replays.

Why It's Not

Rewinding and replaying trauma repeatedly floods your body again and again with stress hormones. It creates deeper habits as you drill into your system that same response, because you are reliving it in the same way, or perhaps more acutely each time you relive it.

There is a tendency to add more details with each rewind, eventually pulling in moments from the past or even moments from the future to truly create a mountain out of a molehill.

Observation Break

Recall a Hot Potato that is still hot.

State it simply.

(NAME)_____hurt/upset/annoyed/disrespected me when they _____.

A. How long did the actual incident (not the aftermath, just what was said or done) last in minutes?

B. How much time have you spent reliving it or actively thinking about it since the incident took place?

Compare A to B. Which was longer?

Has rewinding it made you feel better, more relaxed, and more at ease?

17

PLAYING WITH
HOT POTATOES

In this next section, you are going to PLAY with all the ways we handle Hot Potatoes. Before starting, if you are reading this in the paperback version, please cut out the cards that are printed

on the last three pages of this book. If you are reading an ebook, (or simply prefer) you can download and print the Hot Potato cards from the Online Resources or draw a set.

Crazy, sort-of-related update: Just as I was writing this section near our community pool, I could hear the words, "Hot Potato, Hot Potato" being chanted by a bunch of kids in the pool. Turns out there is a whole game around Hot Potatoes that I never knew existed. You throw a "Hot Potato" to another person, and whoever has it when the music stops loses!!!! No wonder we are

always throwing "Hot Potatoes" to someone else!

We are going to be playing with the different ways we handle Hot Potatoes. I use the word 'play' because it is good to approach it in the mindset of a game to keep things lighthearted and not feel so serious.

YOUR FAVORITE HOT POTATO HANDLINGS

Grab your 12 Hot Potato cards.

- SWEEP IT UNDER THE RUG
- BLAME

- SELF-BLAME
- RUN
- HIDE
- RESEARCH & RULES
- NUMB & DISTRACT
- DAYDREAM & HOPE
- OFFERINGS & SACRIFICE
- FILE
- ENLIST
- REWIND & REPLAY

HOT POTATO GAME #1

For our first game, arrange the Hot Potato cards in order of how often you use each one.

Once arranged, pick up the card of your FIRST most used handling. Study the card and reflect on the questions below:

- How would you change the picture to better represent how you experience it?
- What is a humorous example of using this Hot Potato handling?
- How often do you use this handling?
- In which situations do you tend to use it?
- What do you like about using it?
- What do you not like about using it?
- How is it helpful?
- How is it not helpful?
- How does it create connection?

Do this same thing with each of the remaining cards. Noticing how your answers change.

HOT POTATO GAME #2

Put the cards in order of how much you dislike how other people handle their Hot Potatoes, from most disliked to least disliked.

Starting at the top reflect on these four questions for each:

- What do you think the hurt could be underneath that hot type of Hot Potato handling?
- How do you think that type of handling helps the other person avoid pain?
- What would you prefer they do?
- When have you used this handling, even only in your mind?

HOT POTATO GAME #3

Think of a Hot Potato. Write it down with no details, just give a title like "The time my husband forgot my birthday," or "The time my daughter said I was a terrible mother when I told her she couldn't go on a trip this month."

Now shuffle the cards and start at the top. For each card, describe the thoughts you would have for each of those handlings. Using the example above about the daughter, some thoughts might be:

Sweep It Under the Rug: "I shouldn't feel like this; I don't want her to know she can upset me. I'm the mother, after all."

Blame: "What a horrible daughter she is?"

Self-blame: "Boy, did I screw that up!"

Run: "I've got to get some time away from her, wish I could."

Hide: "I'm never getting in that position again. I'll have her dad make these decisions from now on. Let him be the bad guy."

Reasons & Rules: "I should read that book about raising more respectful kids."

Numb & Distract: "I'm just going to finish watching the new series that just got released. She'll get over it."

Daydream & Hope: "When she grows up, I'll finally get the respect I deserve."

Offerings & Sacrifices: "Maybe I should let her go. Or maybe I could take her out to dinner to make up for it."

File: "She is getting difficult. I'm not going to say anything now, but watch to see if this is something that continues."

Enlist: "I should see if Stacy thinks my daughter overreacted."

Rewind & Replay: "Did she really say that? I can't believe she said that. God, I wish I could stop thinking about this; it's so upsetting."

And so ends our first part of the tour. During this exploration, we looked at all the things we choose to do instead of saying OUCH! at that precise moment.

By leaving the Hot Potato burning, no matter which of the various handlings we use, the result will always end in disconnection.

But there is good news—the second part of our trip offers a simple, yet effective, way to dissolve these.

PART TWO

When I present this material live and get to the end of all these methods we use to keep holding onto Hot Potatoes, the next question I am always asked is, "Is there something I can do instead?"

There are so many ways we are taught to deal with Hot Potatoes in life. "More precise communication," or "Fully expressing your needs," or "Finding the right partner/friend/ associate." These are all helpful guidelines and possibilities for changing your external environment, but let's look at some ways to cool the Hot Potato entirely.

Before we do anything else, though, let's cover one of the most important points—choice.

18

FREEDOM TO CHOOSE

The truth is you might NOT want to let the hurt go.

If anyone has ever tried to force you or guilt you into letting go of something, I'm sorry. It needs to be YOUR choice. If you aren't ready to look at the *possibility* of cooling down some Hot Potatoes, set this book aside and come back to it if and when you're ready.

Please know it is absolutely okay if you're not ready yet.

TURNING POINT: Ready to look?

So many times, people talk about being free as something you MUST do! "Break free from your past!" or "Let go of that already." After everything I've been through, the research that I've done, and the "releasing sessions" I do, I am 100% certain that freedom is utterly dependent on choice.

I once had a parakeet named Petey. He lived his whole life in a cage. I didn't like it. It felt like he wasn't free. So, as soon as I brought him home, I wanted him to feel free to fly around the

house and enjoy his wings (I was always sort of envious that birds could fly). I would leave the door to his cage open, hoping he would fly out, but he remained defiantly in his cage. Finally, one day, I decided to force him out. I reached into his cage and tried to scoop him up. He did everything he could to avoid me. After eventually catching him, I excitedly opened my hand, expecting him to fly around with joyful glee. But he flew straight back to his cage. Perplexed, I repeated the action, and so did Petey. I still remember the trauma (to both of us).

After many unsuccessful attempts, I changed tactics and left the door of his cage open with his favorite treats in a bowl in the living room. He finally decided it was safe (I'm guessing it took even longer after all the trauma I'd inadvertently caused), and he ventured out and flew around. In time, this became a regular occurrence, and soon he was sitting on my shoulder, especially during dinner time. But he always went home to the safety of his cage.

So, having learned from this, nothing in this book is designed to tell you to do anything. In fact, it might be frustrating to you if you were wanting rules to follow, and instead, you were given different paths to follow. But that is the essence of freedom.

Let's look at why you might actually NOT want to cool any Hot Potatoes you currently have.

As with all the tensions we hold onto, such as hurt, grief, and guilt, we have good reasons for doing this. Even if you say you want to be free of them, you may have hidden mental opposition preventing you from letting go.

If you do not feel free to hold on with no judgment, no blame, or no "musts," you cannot authentically decide to let it go. Decisions require choice. Remember, too, letting go isn't even a yes/no choice. It is more of a sliding scale. You can choose to let go a little or a lot. You can, like Petey, choose when.

It might sound crazy to think you want to hold onto hurt, but as we explored the various types of Hot Potato Handlings, including why they are awesome and why they are not, there are a bunch of really good reasons to hold onto them and keep them hot. Let's look at a few.

19

GOOD REASONS TO HOLD ONTO HURT

STICKY NOTE

The first reason is one I like to call the Sticky Note. A long time ago, I loved to put physical sticky notes all over my office as reminders—do this, do that, don't forget to buy that item.

Having something always in front of you to remind you about what you want to achieve is helpful. It directs our attention and keeps us focused on the future.

We can use this with hurt. We don't ever want to forget the pain we had because we don't want to get hurt again. So, we use the pain itself as a reminder. Let's say a friend shared some personal information about you in a group, which was unexpected and made you feel betrayed—sick to your stomach, even.

When you talk to her about anything, you feel uneasy and uncomfortable. Sharing personal information with other people reminds you of that incident, and you are wary of what you say.

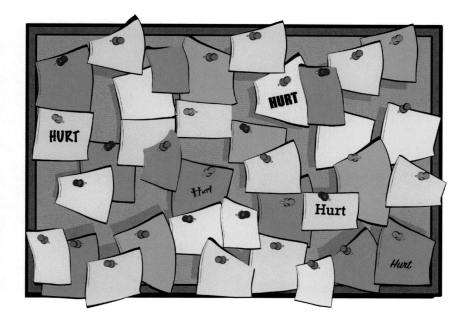

All of this is a way to make sure you are never hurt again.

One of the main differences between a to-do sticky note and one to remind you of pain is that once a to-do is done, you can throw it away. But a reminder of pain never gets removed since it isn't about something specific. Instead, the notes just keep piling up.

With these sticky notes, it is a good idea to evaluate how they are helping you. Are they useful or just cluttering up your mind?

Observation Break

Bring to mind a Hot Potato from your past.

- When did it happen?
- Where were you?
- How many times have you thought about that incident since then?

- When and where did you think about it?
- How does it make you feel or act?
- On a scale of 1 to 10, how much upset did that initially create?
- What would your life be like if you didn't even have the memory of the event?

SUFFERING & PUNISHMENT

When talking with people about letting go of Hot Potatoes, one of the things that often comes up is thinking, "If I let go of the hurt, it will let the other person off the hook, and they will forget what they did." It is sort of like a reverse sticky note, except this time, we want THEM to remember how much hurt they caused.

There is an often quoted saying: "Holding onto anger or resentment is like drinking poison and waiting for the other person to die."

In essence, this is true. But I believe there is a good reason for this. As humans, it's our instinct to help out those that are suffering, particularly when we're very young.

What is your earliest memory of compassion? When have you been compelled to reach out, even to a stranger, to help because you see them and you see their suffering?

Think back to your childhood and see if you can remember not wanting to anger your parents or teachers. Can you find a time when you changed your behavior so as not to annoy them? Isn't it natural?

So, if someone didn't see you in pain and didn't do anything to ease it, then wouldn't it make sense to suffer even MORE to finally gain their attention?

In the same vein, if someone doesn't change their behavior when you're angry or upset, becoming angrier or even MORE upset might do the trick, right?

I had an example of this in a relationship. It's funny when I look back now and see how useless all of it was, but at the time, it seemed to make sense. Towards the end of one of my relationships, I was feeling soooo hurt and so unseen and unloved that I would stay up crying all night. I'd wake up with puffy red eyes, which upset my partner even more. What did I do? I put dark eyeshadow under my eyes to make it even worse!! Can you see from my limited viewpoint how it seemed like it might work? As you might have guessed, it didn't.

The sometimes-unseen aspect of using upset or anger to create a change is there must be a connection or threat. If the person has become the enemy in your eyes and needs to be punished, you have NO connection with them, and, unless you have power over them as an enemy (or parent or employee or someone else holding more power), then there is no threat.

If you are connected with them, you are better able to let them know you are hurting in a way they can receive. You are on the same side of the table. You are a team.

And if they are not in your life or are deceased, what good does holding on to this hurt do?

Observation Break

Who has hurt you and hasn't noticed how much they hurt you?

Are you still letting them know? How?

What would happen if they never realized how much they hurt you?

Who is your hurt hurting?

IDENTITY

When we hold onto hurt for so long, it becomes part of us—our identity. We even use it to bond with others.

I used to tell people that I wanted to get to know me, about my experiences as a teenager with my mother. My hurt over that relationship was a Hot Potato that I carried for so many years. I would get to a certain level of intimacy with a new friend or potential partner, and I would then share my past. Perhaps they would share theirs. It felt close and connecting. What would have happened if I didn't have deep hurt to share, and similarly, what if they didn't have deep hurt to share? Could we have still had a connection?

I am part of a group of women that gathers for online video calls during the week and we share the following:

- What was our high of the week?
- What was our low?
- We answer one of the 36 Questions to Fall in Love (I just love these questions)
- We ask for specific support that we need from the rest of the group

Each week, there is always something new to discuss. Often the high and the low for the week can be the same. It is fascinating the level of intimacy we create. We cry and laugh with one another, even though some of us have never met in person. Even when there is someone new joining the conversation, the connection is just as deep.

Authentic sharing can occur with anyone, at any time, about any subject, regardless of how long you've known them. If the bond is genuine, any discussion can be rewarding and connecting.

Sometimes, though, our hurt is hard to release because we have built an entire life around it. We can feel like the hurt defines us.

One woman I interviewed talked about the hurt she carried from learning her husband preferred men and thinking he simply wanted to marry her to have children. She described how she told so many people her story that it became the label others had for her; "Oh, she's the woman whose husband is gay."

This can happen, too, in support groups. Creating a supportive environment with someone is a gift. Creating an identity or social structure around continuing hurt can prevent the possibility of letting it go.

On the flip side, it can also be something we don't want to let out because it might change how people perceive us or how we see ourselves. This is especially true with childhood trauma or hurt involving events that others would disapprove of or would make you "look" bad.

A personal example of this was when I worked with my former husband. We had moved to another city, and most of my new friends were part of the company we worked with. I held in so much hurt because I didn't want to ruin the illusion that everything in my life was perfect. I wanted to be a role model for our clients and my staff, all the while being constantly hurt from how critical he was with my work, and holding onto it.

Observation Break

Recall a Hot Potato you've had for a long time that you talk about openly and repeatedly with others.

- Who would you be without this Hot Potato in your life?
- How would you tell your life story without that in it? Could you?
- What groups could you NOT be a part of or what friends could you NOT have if you let go of that hurt?
- Who would be upset with you if you let go of the hurt?
- Who would you not be able to connect as closely with, without this hurt?
- What part of you would be lost if you could NEVER talk about this again?

Now recall a Hot Potato that you **don't** want to tell anyone about.

- What would happen to you if others knew?
- How would this change their opinion of you?
- What would your life story be to the world if this were known?

HURT SHOULD LAST BECAUSE . . .

This one is sort of a catch-all. One of the reasons we hold onto hurt is because we think we SHOULD. Think of all the movies you've watched or books you've read where someone has had their feelings hurt, or they've been disrespected or disappointed. What is the typical response?

I just finished watching the video of the Broadway show, *Hamilton*. Both Hamilton and his son died in duels over honor—someone disrespected someone else, and it ended in death. *Romeo and Juliet*, a story retold in so many ways, teaches us that the more you suffer, the more you loved. If you think it only occurs in ancient stories, the tabloids are filled with modern-day stories of hurt, anger, and revenge.

These stories, and thousands of others like them, give us the false impression that hurt should last.

Ever had any of these thoughts?:

- "The more I hurt and the longer I hurt, the more it means that I loved her."
- "If I stop hurting, he will never come back."
- "If I let go, I'm weak, and I'm a doormat."
- "It takes x number of months or years to heal."
- "If I let go, that means I'm wrong."
- "It's all I have left."
- "It gives me the energy to change."
- "If I don't keep hurting, nothing will change."

Observation Break

Find a hurt that is still alive in you—a scalding, burning Hot Potato.

Finish this sentence: I SHOULD still be upset BECAUSE _____?

Come up with as many reasons as you can.

Find two other hurts that are still hurting (big or small) and do the same thing.

Notice if you have a specific reason that's your go-to—is it 100% true?

20

YOUR WILL

O kay, we've now come to the first exercise that can enable the hurt to heal.

The first step is to intentionally decide if you are *willing* to heal, even a tiny bit (remember this is a sliding scale question, not an all or nothing), to let go of the upset, the Hot Potato, the hurt.

Willing is an interesting word. There is a phrase I heard growing up, "Where there's a will, there's a way." This was first expressed in 1640 as, "To him that will, ways are not wanting." What I love about the original one is the idea that "Ways are not wanting." If you have the will (a deliberate or fixed desire or intention), then there are many ways, not just one

way, to accomplish something.

Too often, we wait until we are certain about an outcome before setting an intention. I am asking you to set the intention to do something with your Hot Potatoes, with the belief that the *ways* will not be lacking. They will show up, if not in the exercises of this book, then somewhere else.

To do this, we are going to look at making a clearer, firmer, more "willful" decision. It is an expanded, in-depth pros and cons list. As we saw, there are lots of really good reasons we hold onto hurt, to these Hot Potatoes, but it isn't often that we take the time to fully examine them.

Exercise—The Choice Is Yours

You will need to set aside 10-15 minutes for this.

There are no right or wrong answers. It is simply a more formalized way of answering the question Linda asked me when she said, "Sweetie, what's in it for you?"

First, in one short sentence, write down an action that was taken or words that were said that you didn't expect and didn't want, or a moment where you expected an action to be done or words to be said, and they simply weren't.

Make the sentence super short, such as:
"(NAME)_____ did/said _____ to me. OUCH!"
Or: "(NAME) didn't do/say _____ to me. OUCH!"

> ****You're going to need this sentence for the next chapter and other future exercises—and for ease of reference, we're calling this a HOT POTATO****

Some examples might be:
- Jack didn't text me back. OUCH!

- My mother said I was screwing up my life. OUCH!
- I got fired. OUCH!
- My friend didn't invite me to her party. OUCH!
- My husband told me I was stupid. OUCH!
- My son didn't come home when he said. OUCH!

In the following questions, when I use the word "get," I am using it with the following definition: "succeed in attaining, achieving, or experiencing; obtain." As in, "YAY! I *get* to have ice cream."

Next, answer each of the questions as fully as possible.

DOING:

What do I get to DO by holding onto this Hot Potato?

What do I get to avoid DOING by holding onto this Hot Potato?

What would I get to DO by cooling or transforming this Hot Potato?

What would I get to avoid DOING by cooling or transforming this Hot Potato?

HAVING:

What do I get to HAVE by holding on to this Hot Potato?

What do I get to avoid HAVING by holding on to this Hot Potato?

What would I get to HAVE by cooling or transforming this Hot Potato?

What would I get to avoid HAVING by cooling or transforming this Hot Potato?

EXPERIENCING:

What do I get to EXPERIENCE by holding onto this Hot Potato?

What do I get to avoid EXPERIENCING by holding onto this Hot

Potato?

What would I get to EXPERIENCE by cooling or transforming this Hot Potato?

What would I get to avoid EXPERIENCING by cooling or transforming this Hot Potato?

Upon completion, take a short break.

Now, decide if you want to let go of that hurt, even just a little bit. The answer might be NO, which is totally and absolutely awesome. You can't ever consciously, honestly, and completely let go of something that you don't feel you have a choice over.

So, if it's a NO, set this book aside for now, or find another Hot Potato. It is okay.

But in order to go on, make sure you have a hurt you honestly have the WILL to release, even if only a little bit of it.

TURNING POINT: Do you want to cool a Hot Potato?

21

LET'S COOL THINGS DOWN

There is an energy or feeling that facilitates healing, and that's the energy of compassion.

What is compassion? One of the many definitions of the word is "To empathize with someone who is suffering and to feel compelled to reduce the suffering."

One of the questions I had after reading this definition was, "What do others see as the opposite of compassion?"

Here are some common antonyms for compassion:

- Indifference
- Insensitive
- Aloofness
- Cold-heartedness
- Detachment
- Hatred
- Animosity
- Contempt
- Abhorrence
- Disgust
- Coldness
- Dislike
- Loathing
- Revulsion
- Aversion

When I asked people this question, many simply said the opposite of compassion is judgment. Wow, did that make sense! All of the words above have judgment as the common denominator. Look at these examples:

- Why would you be indifferent towards someone's suffering? They aren't worth noticing.
- Why would you hate someone? They did something very wrong.
- Why do you feel disgust? They are toxic.
- Why are you insensitive to their plight? They deserved what they got.

Oftentimes we turn the judgment towards ourselves.

I never really noticed how much I judged my own hurts and how little compassion I had for myself until I had a physical example of it.

A couple of years ago, I had a painful knee for no apparent reason. I was icing it and hobbling around for days, so I made an appointment with a Reiki healer named Maria Parra, who had helped me in the past and happened to be in town.

When I focused my attention on my knee, my thoughts were:

"What's wrong with me?"

"What did I do to deserve this pain?"

"Damn knee."

"This isn't fair; my knee shouldn't be hurting?"

Can you see how all those questions have judgment built into them?

When Maria touched my knee, what I experienced was nothing

short of a miracle. She put her hands over my knee and I could feel compassion. That is the only way to describe it. It felt like love, acceptance, and the willingness to help.

It was the strangest experience. I don't think she approached me with the idea that there was something wrong with my knee and needed to be *fixed*. It was more like it needed love. And she gave that to me.

From that moment on, I felt no pain in my knee.

This is the space we are going to "hold," a space of "compassion."

There is something important to realize about stress. If you don't stress out about the stress (as in "I don't want to feel like this forever") or replay the stressor (the incident that triggered the stress) it takes a very short time to let the physical response work its way through your body. Between fifteen to ninety seconds, depending on who you are talking to. This makes sense, as bodies need that jolt to move in situations of physical distress.

Experiencing this lesson for the first time is such a vivid memory for me.

As I walked down the street, a text from a man I had dated— and who had ended the relationship—popped up on my screen.

Immediately, I felt a horrible pang of rejection fill my stomach. I couldn't even walk; I stopped, practically doubled over, and started counting to ninety. As I counted, I tried to focus not on resisting or changing or judging how I was feeling, but just being with the pain; accepting it, noticing it, and loving it. After about fifty seconds, the panic and the sick feeling in my stomach was gone.

A few days later, something else triggered the same icky, OUCH! feeling, and tears came flooding out of my eyes. I was afraid they wouldn't stop, but I repeated the same exercise, starting from one. Again, within sixty seconds, it was gone. In that moment, I knew I only needed to experience any emotional pain for up to ninety seconds, then it would subside. It was a moment of such freedom.

I would love for you to experience this freedom too.

So, if you are ready, let's move onto an exercise I like to call, Cooling the Potato.

There are several ways to do this, but since this is a book format, we are going to do a combination of writing and reflecting.

Exercise—Cool the Hot Potato

Make sure you are in a quiet space where you feel comfortable and will be undisturbed. This will take between five and fifteen minutes.

You will be giving yourself the compassion and love you need for your hurt—with no judgment.

You're going to use your imagination and your breath. You should read through the entire exercise before starting it. Or, if you prefer to listen, download a guided observation from the Online Resources.

Also, if you have questions or problems with this, you can always go to the Online Resources for Frequently Asked Questions or to ask one of your own.

There is a lot of attention lately on creating resilience. In physics, resilience is the ability of a material to absorb energy (such as from a blow) and release that energy as it springs back to its original shape. It is similar to a person's ability to bounce back after a jarring setback. This exercise addresses this.

Before starting, take several deep breaths. Then follow the instructions below:

1 Write down the Hot Potato you consciously decided to release in the first exercise—see **The Choice Is Yours exercise in Chapter 20.** It should have looked like this:

"(NAME)_____ did/said _____ to me. OUCH!"

2. Look at the methods of "Holding onto the Hot Potato" you have primarily been using for this. Notice with curiosity, or appreciation, or gratitude how this was a way to reduce or prevent hurt.

3. Notice how that method has disconnected you from the other person or yourself. What did you see?

4. Bring your attention again to the exact moment when that thing was said, or not said; done, or not done.

5. Describe any colors and/or patterns you are seeing.

6. Notice something in that scene you never focused on before. What was it?

7. Notice any surprise you had that this happened. Were you surprised a little or a lot?

8. Describe any sounds. They could be words, but listen to them as simply noise and notice the pitch you are hearing or the loudness. Notice any other sounds in the background and describe them.

9. Are there any sounds you are feeling compelled to make that you didn't at the time, for example, screaming or

yelling? How loud would it be? If you feel comfortable, make that exact sound now or simply take a few moments and imagine yourself making that sound and how it would feel.

10. Describe any physical sensations. Is your body wanting to move in a certain direction or position? How would you move it? If you feel comfortable, for a few minutes move your body in that way or position now or simply imagine yourself doing that and how it would feel.

11. Is there tension or stress in your body related to this? Where is that tension? If you aren't sure, imagine where it *would* be if it were there. Maybe it's in your chest, or stomach, or head, neck, or anywhere else.

If needed, repeat all of the above until you feel better about the incident.

Now for the next part of this exercise, read over the following six steps in advance, as you will be doing them with your eyes closed. There is also a recording at the Online Resources that will lead you through this.

1. Close your eyes and take several deep breaths.

2. Put your hands on the part of your body where you have or imagine the tension is. Hold it gently. As lovingly as you can, say, "I am so sorry this happened" and mean it from the bottom of your heart. Add any other words a person who loves you completely and unconditionally would say to you, to express love and compassion, such as, "I'm here for you" or "I love you" or "We'll figure this out together" or "You aren't alone." Keep saying it over and over until you feel better.

3. Say "Thank you." Thank yourself for giving yourself that compassion from the bottom of your heart. Now breathe in, imagining your breath going directly into that area of your body. If you like, visualize this oxygen as loving, healing light.

4. Now exhale gently and imagine you are lovingly releasing your tension and sensation, plus imagine all the sounds or images or tension ebbing away. Don't force it. If any emotion comes up, keep focusing on the area of your body with love and compassion, as the father from the video I mentioned in Chapter 3 did with his daughter.

5. Keep doing this, breathing love and compassion into your hurt area for about ninety seconds, or until the intensity of that moment diminishes or leaves altogether.

6. With your eyes closed, bring a smile to your face that goes all the way to your eyes. Holding on to your smile, slowly open your eyes.

You can do this over and over again any time you are feeling upset.

But what if it doesn't diminish? There are two paths you can take.

1. Look again at the hurt and see if there is another way you are handling it—perhaps blame or self-blame—that you hadn't previously acknowledged, and start at the beginning of the exercise to Cool the Hot Potato.

   or

2. There might be another hurt filed in the same file folder, so to speak. See if anything else similar comes to mind and start at the beginning of the exercise to Cool the Hot Potato.

Then, anytime you start to feel tense or upset, come back to this exercise and redo it. Once you get a sense that you can cool a Hot Potato, all of them will be less scary, less painful.

It is such a relief to know that whatever life throws at you, you can consciously release it in a short time.

Having this superpower gives you the freedom to experience life with an open heart and a sense of fearlessness, because now you're not so worried about the pain life brings.

PART THREE

This part of the book will help you dissolve more than just one hurt. It is going to show you a way to dissolve what is underneath it, so life is less OUCHY! altogether. We are going to move away from the stories, teachings, and light observations to deeper internal work.

I'm going to give you step-by-step instructions to really **O**bserve what's **U**nderneath, **C**reating the **H**urt.

The steps are written as though you are with me in person or at one of my workshops. It will take two to three hours of uninterrupted time, not only reading through it, but also working your way through the many exercises that will help you organize your thoughts.

The material and exercises in this part may feel like too much to digest or appear overwhelming if you aren't actually completing the exercises as you go.

If you aren't in a position to set aside the time right now to gather up the materials and do the exercises, you have two options:

1. Simply read over the material and save all the exercises for a time in the future.

    or

2. Just come back to this book when you are ready to explore more.

A personal example of this was when I read the best-selling book, *Getting Things Done: The Art of Stress-Free Productivity,* by David Allen. I read the book several times, but then never organized anything. Reading it gave me hope though, and one weekend, I decided I was ready to spend the two full days it took to implement every instruction in Allen's book, which included cleaning up over 5,000 emails in my inbox—yikes!

You can do the same; read it all and then come back when you are ready to delve in deeper. There are still insights you might glean.

What You'll Need to Get Started

If you are going to complete the exercises in this part of the book, there are some things you will need:

- **Time**: Set aside two to three hours where you can be undisturbed and be able to fully focus.
- **Materials**: Print out the worksheets from the Online Resources or have plenty of pieces of blank paper to write on. It can be a journal, notebook, or simply loose pages. You could also use a blank computer page if you have no access to paper; however, there is just something that seems more connecting if you write by hand.
- **Optional**: A friend to do this with.

TURNING POINT—Are you ready to begin?

Either:

I'm ready! I have the time and materials -or- Nope, not ready. I'll come back to this when I am -or- I'll just read it now and maybe do the exercises later.

22

IN WHICH STATE DO YOU WANT TO LIVE?

The first exploration is to learn which *state or states* you want to live in.

Now you might ask, "What do you mean, like the state of California?" That's not exactly the definition I'm going to be using, but there are some similarities. For example, living in the state of California gives you access to beaches, beautiful weather, and a certain vibe. And you can make choices because you live in that state, like throwing an impromptu party outdoors in December. This is something you couldn't do if you lived in Norway, unless you had a decent set of thermal underwear.

I'm using this definition of the word 'state': "mode or condition of being." The state you are in determines how you will respond to external events.

Let's take water as an example.

In a solid state, it doesn't move much. It can hold someone up as they skate, or it can crack, subsequently hurting someone.

In a liquid state, it flows and moves. It makes up 90% of our bodies. It allows certain creatures to live in it, yet can drown others.

In a gaseous state, it can fly and float. It can create clouds and reflect light and create rain.

All of these different states create different capacities.

The same is true for us.

If you are in a state of peace and someone insults you, you wouldn't attack them. If you are in a state of fear and someone offers you a beautiful gift, you might refuse it. If you are in a state of anger and someone bumps into you, you might be annoyed, but if you're in a calm state, you'd probably accept it was an accident and go about your day.

The difference between us and water is *we can choose to change the state we are in*.

EXERCISE—Find Your Favorite States

First, notice how you are feeling right now.

Next, think of something someone did to you that still hurts (something small, as this is just a demonstration).

- Did they hurt your feelings, disrespect you, annoy you?
- Did it disappoint you?
- How did it make you feel?
- What are all the details leading up to it?

Notice your current state.

- Are you tense, angry, and are you breathing faster?
- What would you NOT be able to do in this state? (e.g., give someone a hug or help a stranger)

Now, think of something that you are deeply grateful for. Imagine it as though it is happening right now. Spend a few minutes reliving that moment, smile at it.

Again, notice your state.

- Are you more relaxed, happier, and perhaps more at peace?
- Has some tension in your body dissipated?
- What could you do in this state that you couldn't if you were upset?

In all the times I covered this topic in workshops and with clients, I've NEVER heard someone say, "I want to live in a suffering state, I want to be worried, I want to be afraid, I want to be jealous, I want to be angry." People will say they want to be in a state of love, intimacy, joy, or something similar.

There are certain states that YOU prefer to be in, where you are being "your best self" as some people say. These are different from person to person, so we are going to gain clarity on states you choose to be in. It isn't that you will always be in that state. It's like if you live in the state of Utah, you might visit the state of New York to see your parents. The difference between physical states and states of being is that we generally make a conscious choice to fly to a different state, yet we instantly flip from calm to anger without any form of control.

The first step is to write down eight states you want to be in. The order is irrelevant. You can use the list below for inspiration, but please add some of your own:

- Acceptance
- Affection
- Authenticity
- Awareness
- Beauty
- Celebration
- Clarity
- Compassion
- Competence
- Connection
- Consciousness
- Cooperation
- Creativity
- Curiosity
- Ease
- Empathy
- Equality
- Faith
- Flow
- Freedom
- Generosity
- Grace
- Gratitude
- Happiness
- Harmony
- Honesty
- Hope
- Inclusion
- Independence
- Inspiration
- Integrity
- Intimacy
- Joy
- Laughter

THE POWER OF OUCH!

- Love
- Peace
- Play
- Presence

- Productivity
- Thoughtfulness
- Truth
- Understanding

Next, you are going to be comparing each of these dispositions with the question, "Does it feel better to be in state A or B?" So, for example, if you created the following list:

A. *Love*
B. *Faith*
C. *Joy*
D. *Generosity*
E. *Curiosity*
F. *Thoughtfulness*
G. *Happiness*
H. *Peace*

First, ask yourself, "Does it feel better to be in a state of Love or be in a state of Certainty?" Imagine yourself being Loving and notice how it feels, and then imagine yourself being Certain. For me, the answer would be Loving.

Next, take the one that feels best and compare it to C. (For me, I would compare, "Does it feel better to be in a state of Love or a state of Joy?)

Then, take the winner from that comparison and compare it to D. Then, take the winner from that comparison and compare it to E, and so on until you are finished.

You will now have your chosen first state. Eliminate it from the list and do the entire exercise again to get your second favorite state. Then, eliminate that state from the list and do it all again to ascertain your third state.

By the end, you will have your top three favorite states. Write them down, as you will be using them all throughout the next section.

What is your favorite state?   _____

What is your second favorite state?   _____

What is your third favorite state?   _____

But before we go on, take a moment, and imagine a life where you were living a life solely in these three states. What would that be like?

23

THE BLACK BOX

What makes something OUCHY! to a person is simply the mental mechanisms they have. It's like our mind is a machine, and there's an input and an output. All sorts of external stimuli from the world go in, and out come Hot Potatoes ("bad" experiences) or Daisies ("good" expriences). I like to call this a Black Box.

WHAT'S INSIDE THE BLACK BOX?

There is a lot going on inside that box, and how it got there is something I love to talk about in workshops. What is important now though, is learning to change what comes out of the box to be more in line with the experience of life we want to have.

Often, we try to change what goes INTO the box in order to have the experience we want. We try to change what other people say or do or even think. But oftentimes, the simpler and more effective thing to do is look inside the box and see if there's a glitch.

I recently upgraded my new phone and I finally went through all my apps. About a third of them didn't even work anymore. Because of the new operating system, many of the apps weren't up to date. Another third weren't useful because I no longer live in New York, and they were location-based, so were completely useless here in Puerto Rico.

This happens with the "apps" in our minds too. They become obsolete or broken. They slow down our mental processes and take up space, falsely giving us a feeling that they have value.

So, instead of trying to change the input the world gives us, we are going to look at the "apps" creating the output.

We are going to delve into them right now, but be warned, it isn't necessarily fun.

This is similar to confronting all the things you have thrown into your junk drawer or the thousands of photos on your phone that are out of focus or blurry. When you first open your drawer or photo gallery, it can seem completely overwhelming and you don't know where to begin. But, once you start, there is something therapeutic about the process and the end result leaves you feeling clearer, calmer, and more in control.

THE POWER OF OUCH!

So, this last section is about organizing the mess in our minds—our Black Box. There are four common types of "apps" in the box that are ripe for either an upgrade or deletion.

Meanings

Expectations

Stories

Strategies

I call this the **M.E.S.S.**

24

LET'S ORGANIZE THE M.E.S.S.

After each topic—**Meanings, Expectations, Stories,** and **Strategies**—there are exercises to help you transform your thinking. It's going to be like reorganizing a messy closet.

Nowadays, you can't talk about organizing without referencing Marie Kondo and her book, *The Life-Changing Magic of Tidying Up.*

She teaches us to only keep those things that spark joy. Now, when I'm organizing my closet, I'll hold the dress, shoes, or hat up to my heart and see how it makes me feel. I'll see if it "sparks joy" (Weird, but it works. You can actually feel if something sparks joy). If I feel it doesn't spark joy, I let it go with gratitude, and if possible, give it to someone else who might need it or want it. When I first read her book and was organizing my apartment, I could see the same reasons I held onto physical things were very similar to the reasons I held onto mental things. I was attached to the past or worried about the future. It was such an eye-opener.

Another similarity between cleaning out the M.E.S.S. in your mind and the mess in your closet, is that it will look a lot messier before it is more organized. If you are just reading it, without doing any of the exercises, it can make you feel worse. If this happens, just come back when you are ready.

I also like to keep in mind this quote from Carl Jung: "One does **not** become **enlightened** by imagining figures of light, but by making the darkness conscious. The latter procedure, however, is disagreeable and therefore **not popular**."

We are going to be diving into the darkness of our "Black Box." By darkness, I don't mean evil or bad, just not lit up, not seen.

To make it less "disagreeable," each section will follow the same format:

1. A short explanation of the topic.
2. Any examples or instructions for the exercises.
3. The actual exercises. (You can download PDF worksheets from the Online Resources)

If you have any questions or get overwhelmed, you can visit the FAQ section at the Online Resources or write to me at me@ sondrahamon.com.

TURNING POINT—Are you ready to start organizing?

25

MEANINGS

Humans are constantly trying to find meanings. We use words and symbols all day long and would be lost if we didn't know exactly what they meant. Our brains are accustomed to seeing things and coming up with a meaning. We see the letters "B," "O," and "X," and we immediately think, "That means a thing

BOX

THE POWER OF OUCH!

that you can fill with items," or "That means people hitting each other with big gloves inside a ring which is, in fact, square." These two definitions are so different, but we figure them out by understanding the context in which they are written.

How many times as children did we get corrected or scolded for not knowing what something means?

This can get us in trouble in relationships, as unlike a word, which might have between only two or twenty meanings (and they are listed in the dictionary), actions, motivations, and intentions of other people can be limitless.

One of my favorite examples is when I left some laundry on the bed instead of putting it away. Later in the day, I came back to discover that my husband had put everything in the closet. My mind latched onto the meaning that he was impatient with me and thought the bedroom was messy with the clothing stacked up and laying out, and that I was a bad wife. OUCH!

Did I know that for sure? Hell no! With that meaning in my mind, I could have used any one of my favorite Hot Potato handlings, which—for this incident—would have been self-blame. A lot of times, when I tell this story, people will say, "Aw, that's so sweet. It just means that he loves you."

It's so fascinating. I had specific meanings about him and about myself, while other people had completely different ones.

When we discussed it later, my husband clarified, "I just wanted to be helpful. I thought you were busy." He could easily have said, "I wanted to take a nap, so I needed the bed cleared," or one of a thousand other things. No matter what he says, I am still going to find myself thinking, "What does this mean?"

All of this gets us into a never-ending loop where we start to look for meanings within meanings and meaning about ourselves.

Growing up, one of my favorite quotes from Edgar Allan Poe was:

Is all that we see or seem
But a dream within a dream?

It is more like a meaning of a meaning.

For example, let's say a friend forgets your birthday and doesn't call. Instant Hot Potato! So, you search for the reason for not being called, such as "she forgot," and almost immediately conclude, "I don't matter to her anymore," which then means, "She isn't a good friend," and leads to, "I shouldn't be so trusting."

Another person might have a chain that looks like this: a friend forgets to call on their birthday. Hot Potato! That means, "she didn't want to call," which means, "I must have upset her," which then means, "I'm a bad friend."

As you can see, our thoughts are scary, or at least they scare us. Every meaning we don't like hurts like hell.

We can't run away from our thoughts, so we need to stop going down these rabbit-holes. But how? The answer is to wake up to the meanings we are assigning.

For the upcoming exercise, we are going to dive into your meanings and examine them. It will help you clean up the meanings that are creating the hurt.

In the same way we are given the meaning of words by others, the same is true of all meanings. You can choose which meaning of a word makes sense in a sentence, and you can choose which meaning makes sense for your life and the game you're playing.

Going back to the word "BOX," if you are into fighting, the word means a type of sport. If you are playing baseball, it means the area where the hitter stands. In soccer, it is a penalty area.

You can give meaning based on what game you're playing.

But how do you choose? We are going to use your three favorite states to guide us—refer to the Find Your Favorite States exercise in Chapter 22.

Preparing for the Exercise

I recommend that you download the entire worksheet for this exercise from the Online Resources.

You are going to need a Hot Potato that you have already cooled down, as this won't work as easily if the potato is still piping hot.

Step 1: For ease, let's use the situation from the Cooling the Hot Potato exercise in Chapter 21. You will either be using:

"(NAME) did/said ____ to me. OUCH!"

or

"(NAME) didn't do/say ____ to me. OUCH!"

As a sample, I'm going to be using **Brandon replied to my loving, expressive text with only a thumbs-up emoji, OUCH!**

Step 2: You'll be writing down all the meanings you have about **the other person**.

This means:
He doesn't have time for me.
He doesn't like me.
He is rude.
He isn't very communicative.

Step 3: You'll be adding some crazy meanings.

This means:
He is being held hostage by a terrorist and is unable to type because they cut one of his thumbs off.
He has amnesia and is wandering around NYC lost.

Step 4: You'll be working out what this means about **you**.

This means:
I'm not interesting enough.
I'm not sexy enough.
I'm doing something wrong.
I shouldn't have sent that text.

Step 5: And yes, you'll be coming up with some crazy meanings about you too.

This means:
I am going to be left alone to die.
I will grow old with only cats as my friends.
No one will ever ever ever love me.

Step 6-8: Then you're going to use one of your three favorite states and focus on the meanings each state generates about the other person, you, or life.

Notice how the different states of being result in vastly different meanings and conclusions.

Using the same example: **Brandon replied to my loving, expressive text with only a thumbs-up emoji.**

Favorite State —Joy:

Yay! It means he's got my text! It is so amazing that technogloy connects people that are far apart.

Second Favorite State—Faith:
It means life is happening for me.
He is doing exactly what he should be doing.

Third Favorite State—Love:
It means I get to keep expressing myself lovingly and he gets to express himself efficiently. I love that.

The final step is to consciously chose your meanings.

Now that you've seen an example, let's do the exercise.

EXERCISE—Meanings

(Remember that a worksheet for this can be downloaded from the Online Resources)

1. Write down your Hot Potato:
    (NAME)_____ did/said ____ to me. OUCH!"
    Alternative: (NAME)_____ didn't do/say ____ to me. OUCH!

2. Write down all the meanings you have about the other person.

3. Write down some crazy meanings about them.

4. Write down what this means about you.

5. Write down some crazy meanings about you.

6. What is your favorite state _____?
    In this state, what meanings would you have about the other person, yourself or life in general?

7. What is your second favorite state _____?
    In this state, what meanings would you have about the other person, yourself or life in general?

8. What is your third favorite state _____?

9. In this state, what meanings would you have about the other person, yourself or life in general?

10. You should now have a long list of meanings. Which of these meanings feel right? Which ones "spark joy"?

All the meanings that don't "spark joy" had their place at one time, so can you let them go with gratitude, the same way you let go of an old warm fuzzy sweater that you don't even like anymore? Gently cross out the ones you want to let go of, drawing a line through them with gratitude for them having been there to provide you with safety or certainty or control in the past.

Now here's something rather out of the box to think about— **do you actually need a meaning at all?** What if there was no meaning for that incident? What would that be like? Can you imagine all the extra creative energy you'd have if you weren't spending all your time looking for meaning in everything?

26

EXPECTATIONS

Next, we are going to move on to expectations. The definition of 'expect' is: "to consider probable or certain."

First, let me clearly say that I'm not one of those people who say you should get rid of all your expectations or that expectations are "bad." Over the years, I have spent a lot of time interviewing people about expectations, and I want to share one of my favorites. It was an interview with R.T. Stokes, author of the book *The Relentless Rise* and a former member of the U.S. Navy's submarine fleet.

I was asking for volunteers to interview about expectations, and R.T. wrote to me excitedly, saying that he was passionate about the topic and wanted to participate. I expected he was going to — like so many others I had interviewed — say, "You shouldn't have expectations," "Expectations are the cause of all disappointment," etc. I mean, even Shakespeare said, "Expectation is the root of all heartbreak." When I spoke to R.T. though, he started by emphatically saying, "You MUST have expectations!!"

The way he described it made so much sense. If you were going

to go way down under the ocean in what seems like a large tin tube, and be subject to hundreds if not thousands of pounds of pressure per square inch, then you need to have an expectation that it will hold the pressure and keep you safe and dry. When I looked at expectations that way, I realized we are all swimming in a sea of expectations. I expect the floor to hold my weight when I get out of bed in the morning. I expect that my mail is going to be delivered. I expect that if I deposit money in the bank, I can withdraw it at a later date. The list goes on and on and on. I realized after talking to R.T. that I couldn't even function without expectations.

But he also said— "If you're standing out in the rain, getting wet, expecting not to get wet, there's something wrong."

I am sure some of you will remember a pilot by the name of

Chesley "Sully" Sullenberger III, who landed the plane in the East River in Manhattan, making headlines around the world. Tom Hanks portrayed him in the film, *Sully,* about the incredible incident.

Now, R.T. was one of the people investigating how a plane could run into a flock of birds and lose the use of both engines. The investigation team didn't deny that it happened. Can you imagine them all saying, "There's no way that could happen?" Instead, they all saw that a flock of birds could take down a plane.

I think this is where we get caught up in the problems of expectations.

We create an idea in our mind, and we repeat it, and we repeat it, and we repeat it, again and again, until it becomes an expectation. It's the same way the sun always rises. And the same way that thousands of planes were able to fly and NOT crash into the East River in Manhattan. Then something happens, and rather than looking at what DID happen, we say, "But it couldn't happen." The investigators had to look at the reality of the situation—a flock of birds can cause engine failure.

It is the same as the example of the uselessness of standing out in the middle of the rain expecting not to get wet.

Let me give an example of how this might happen in a relationship. Your partner leaves dirty dishes in the sink. Prior to this, you've had the same repetitive image of a clean sink— you expected it to be spotless and uncluttered every time you looked at it. Now all of a sudden, it's filled with DIRTY DISHES, and lo and behold, a Hot Potato is born!

Preparing for the Exercise

I recommend that you download the entire worksheet for this exercise from the Online Resources.

You are going to need a Hot Potato that you have already cooled down, as this won't work as easily if the potato is still piping hot.

We are going to use this example so you can better understand the exercise: *My mother didn't welcome me home after my trip. OUCH!*

In the first step, you will be noticing the expectation at the heart of this Hot Potato—and describe exactly what you DID expect to happen. Write out the entire expectation. Throughout this guidebook, I've purposefully had you avoid details but for this, please write out ALL the visible and audible details that are part of your expectation, not just generalities.

I expected she would open the door with a big smile that I was home. Give me a big hug. Smile at me some more. Put her hand on my arm and bring me to the kitchen where she had cookies waiting. I expected the first thing she would do is ask me how my trip was and then listen to every adventure with appreciation and interest.

Next, you will look for things that happened that match those expectations, even if they aren't specific but in the realm of what you wanted to experience.

Look to see if any of it happened. Really hunt for all the points that you may not have noticed at the time.

- Was the house where you expected it to be? Did it still have a door on it?
- Did she give you a hug, or was it a loving pat on the back instead?
- Did she smile at any point?
- Did she have any food laid out for you in the kitchen—cookies or otherwise? Was there food in the refrigerator?
- Did she ask you any questions about any subject?

- If she didn't ask questions, did she give you her attention when you spoke, even if only for a little while?

Now explore where each one of the unmet expectations came from. Where have you seen each one before?

- From that person? Maybe that is what they did all the time.
- In other situations? Maybe that is what your best friend's mother does.
- From the media? Maybe you see that in TV shows.
- In your mind? Maybe you just really want that to happen.
- In your ideal scenario? Maybe you see a vision of a perfect welcoming.
- Simply because it "should"? All those other reasons.

Notice that in your Hot Potato, your expectations weren't met. What you thought was probable or certain, wasn't probable or certain.

Notice the difference between your expectation and reality.

It is always helpful to have your expectations match reality. As Byron Katie said, "When I argue with reality, I lose—but only 100 percent of the time."

The last step will be rewriting the expectation to match reality. It can help to start with the word "Sometimes," as in, "Sometimes mothers open the door and don't give a hug."

EXERCISE—Expectations

1. Write down your Hot Potato.
2. Write all the specific details of what you expected.
3. Next, search for things that actually met your expectations.
4. Where did these expectations come from? When and where have you seen it?

- With other people?
- In other situations?
- In the media?
- In your ideal scenario?
- Simply because it "should"?

5. Notice the difference between your expectations and reality.

6. Create and write down a modified expectation that now more closely matches reality. Remember, it helps to start with the word "Sometimes."

Breaking down the unmet expectations causing us pain can help us see more clearly.

We can see what did happen the way we expected them to, which is typically soooo much more than the things that didn't go the way we expected.

We can then reset our expectations so that unmet ones match reality. Just like the plane in the East River, we can't make any change if we are stubbornly thinking something "should" be a certain way when it demonstrably isn't.

Denying reality or "arguing" with reality disconnects us from life and the people in it. It also prevents loving solutions and churns out even more Hot Potatoes.

27

STORIES

Another big part of the M.E.S.S. that is ripe for review and deletion is stories. I have absolutely no idea why for humans, stories are **so** important, but I know they are. We love stories. We spend hours reading stories, and we pay money to watch stories, and we're trying to create a story out of our lives all the time.

I hope you know by now that there is nothing in the book I haven't previously explored with others and myself. So, it's not like I don't intimately know this particular mechanism.

Let me give you an example. A partner once yelled at me, "Everything you touch turns to shit." OUCH! That hurt! Rather than say anything, I took it in and started weaving it into my story.

I remembered all the years I had spent helping him create his passion, and I remember the times he'd said something similar that were "red flags." I remembered all that I had given up to help with his project, and I imagined all the things I could have done with my time. The story was supposed to be that after all the sacrifice, he would notice what a wonderful person I was, and love me with all his heart, so I would feel loved, safe, and secure.

In this story, I was the suffering VICTIM, waiting for him to

change, to become the partner I had imagined he could be, and rescue me from the life of loneliness and disconnection.

So here is this poor guy, who, in a moment of frustration, blurts out something very hurtful. That statement was so way off-script, though. And unfortunately for him, it was a story in which he had no editorial control.

Let's just use the above example and see what happens if I change the story.

What if the story I told and the part I played were different? He says exactly the same hurtful thing to me, but this time my role is the GUIDE:

"Wow, that hurt. He must be in pain and stressed out. He must really be hurting inside to say something so hurtful to me. I wonder if there is anything I can do to help him? What does he need to not hurt so much? He isn't always like this, so something must have triggered him. I am a kind and loving partner, and my heart goes out to him. I want to help him. I am going to stay in a state of love and peace to allow him the space to work this out."

Or my role could be the HERO:

"OUCH! I don't like this. This isn't feeling good and certainly not what I imagine for my life. I am so grateful to have just learned what I don't want. What a great insight! I'll use this as a clue for what I do want to be. I'll learn to be clear with myself and with others about this. I'm so happy I experienced this. I'm going to use this to remind myself and others to share how we want to experience life."

See how you can change your story and your role in it.

It actually goes a step further. I was once on a group call with one of the amazing teachers from O&O Academy. During the call, she listened to a man talking about how he had done almost exactly what I described above. There was a woman he was dating who was unkind and upsetting to him (he probably used harsher words). He described the story he told himself and that when he changed the story, he felt better. Our teacher replied, "That is good, better to tell yourself a better story, but do you need a story at all?" That rocked me. I realized that without complusively needing to fit everything into a story, it is so much easier to see things as they are.

So What Part Are You Playing?

I love Don Miller. If you haven't read his books, he talks about the power of stories and how to use them in business—my favorite is *Building A Story Brand*.

He breaks down the theory of stories into really understandable parts. The components of stories are something that has been studied since the time of the ancient Greeks. But Don makes it fun.

If you look at most stories, you will always have these four types of characters: victim, hero, villain, guide.

Victim—the person being harmed that needs to be saved by someone, think Lois Lane, tied to a railroad track, being rescued by Superman.

Hero—the person who eventually saves the day. The hero starts out weak, with self-doubts or inadequate skills. They transform themselves and overcome barriers (both internal and external); rescuing the victim, or solving the problem.

Villain—the person that is wreaking all the havoc. The villain is usually somebody who had challenges as a hero might, but decides to get revenge and inflict hurt on others.

If you have seen the movie Joker, you will see a strong example of someone having a challenge and deciding to get revenge, rather than transform.

Guide—the one who points the hero in the right direction. The guide isn't emotionally involved in the outcome.

The guide doesn't change, remaining the same throughout the entire story.

They exist, as the name suggests, to guide the hero, presenting alternatives and a path to choose. Think of Michael Caine's role as Alfred in the movie, *Batman*. And, of course, Yoda: "Guide you, I will."

When I work with people on this aspect of the mind, so many say that they are both the victim and the hero, with each one battling for dominance within them. And yes, it is true. It certainly feels this way for many. Which one will prevail?

In addition to these characters, the stories have to have conflict, plus a challenge, and inevitably a resolution.

What happens when we try to fit everything into a story? It causes us to look for conflict because that's what is always at the heart of a good story. Stories cause "good" and "bad," and "right," and "wrong. "

Here's the all-important question—Do you *need* these stories in your life and your relationships?

I always tell people, if somebody ever made a movie in which boy meets girl, boy falls in love with the girl, girl falls in love with the boy, and they lived happily ever after, the movie would flop at the box office. No one would pay to see it. Would you?

Do we need this in our relationships to make them interesting? Do we need the conflict and the tension with the other person? Do we need to be the victim or the hero in the story of our relationships?

If we wanted to experience tension and conflict, couldn't we just go and see a movie? We could simply watch *The Notebook* and cry our eyes out if we wanted, or *Titanic*, or whatever the current movie is that tells the tale of the triumph of love over insurmountable odds, then walk out of the movie theater and happily get on with our lives.

Or if we want to create our own stories, remember that we are the sole scriptwriter and therefore can write them any way we choose!

Preparing for the Exercise

I recommend that you download the worksheet for this exercise from the Online Resources.

You are going to need a Hot Potato that you have already cooled down, as this won't work as easily if the potato is still piping hot.

This exercise is pretty simple; just remember to let your imagination run free when you are creating a new story in step three.

EXERCISE—Stories

1. Choose a Hot Potato in your life that you have already cooled.
2. Answer these questions:

    ■   List out all the people involved with this Hot Potato.

    ■   Which part are you playing? Victim, Villain, Hero, or Guide

    ■   Are you trying to get someone else to save you? Who?

    ■   Are you the one who has been hurt and wants to hurt someone back?

    ■   Are you the one who is going to transform this pain into your three favorite states?

    ■   Are you wisely guiding the hero on the journey you have already taken?

    ■   Who is the hero in your story?

    ■   What is the conflict?

    ■   What has to happen for you to be happy with this story?

    ■   List ten other ways you could be happy with this story.

    ■   Which stories feel best to you?

3. Now, write a new short story about this Hot Potato as if you were living it, feeling it, and reacting to it in your three favorite states in the role you want to play.

It is extraordinary to realize how easy it is to transform your life simply by changing your story.

28

STRATEGY

The last part of the M.E.S.S. is Strategy. The definition of *strategy* I'm using is "the art of planning and directing overall military operations and movements in a war or battle." The definition of *war* that I've selected is "a struggle or competition between opposing forces for a particular end."

I don't know about you, but I was a GREAT strategist when it came to relationships! I had an advisory council (my girlfriends), I had surveillance (social media), and I had handbooks (the vast number of books I read). I was constantly honing my skills at getting people to do what I wanted them to, regardless of whether they wanted to or not.

It is really about control.

Let's look at it from the bigger picture of actual war. In wars between nations, there would never be a reason for two countries to be at war if each country behaved exactly as the other wanted; it just wouldn't make sense. The same applies to individuals.

In really broad terms, the reason that people go to war either

overtly or covertly is:

1. Scarce Resources—needed to survive and thrive

Countries might say, "You won't let us have the water, land, or oil we need to live!!!" And they go to war.

People might say, "I can't have the attention I need if you are looking at your phone." And they go to "war."

2. Ideals—Ideas We Value

A country might say, "Our social structure is better than yours. You need to follow our laws and customs. Our religion is the only true one." And they go to war.

People say, "My opinions, habits, values, judgments, preferences, lifestyle, reaction, emotions, thoughts, actions, and attitudes are better than yours and the only 'right' ones to have." And they go to "war."

3. Future Fears—Losing Essential Resources or Being Made to Betray Ideals

A country might say, "Everything is fine now, but in the future, you might try to take my resources or force me to behave contrary to my ideals." So, they go to war.

People may say, "Everything is fine now, but in the future, I might lose what I need from you or be forced to act contrary to my ideals." So, they go to "war."

I used to be fascinated with the book *The Art of War*. I read every single English translation. I even had a copy of the original Chinese writing.

One point that stood out was, "All warfare is based on deception." Military leaders use deception, distraction, and force to conquer their enemies.

Often we don't realize who we are treating as an enemy. Anytime you're using force, deception, distraction, or similar army tactics on another person, you've unknowingly and unconsciously made them your enemy, even if it's someone you love. Then, we wonder why they respond the way they do.

This last exercise is going to have us shine a light on our goals, our enemies, and our strategies.

Since the topic of this guide is relationships and not oil, land, or air rights, that is where we are going to look.

Preparing for the Exercise

First, find a Hot Potato you've cooled. I'll use this as an example:

My best friend shared a secret of mine—OUCH!

Second, answer all the questions. I'll share sample answers.

■ What is it you want to "have" in your relationship with that person? There are two definitions of the word "have"; one means to "possess," and the other is to "experience." Since you never actually possess the other person in a relationship, the only way to "have" a relationship is to "experience" it.

I want to have those moments where we are just laughing so hard we fall off our chairs.

■ How are you trying to change them?

I want her to be more careful with what she says to people about me.

■ What ideals of theirs are unacceptable to you?

That there's no such thing as confidentiality.

■ What are you worried they will take away from you?

My respect in the community if everyone knows everything about me.

■ How do you worry they will try to make you behave in a way that is contrary to your ideals?

She's always urging me to be as open as she is, which is beyond my comfort level.

■ What do you think they will try to take away that is scarce and needed for you to survive and thrive? Is it really scarce?

Respect. It feels scarce, but probably really isn't.

■ How do you try to control her?

I get mad and don't talk to her for months at a time.

Next you will take several deep breaths.

The last step is to simply write out hwo you would say exactly what you want and why, as though that other person were **totally and completely** on board as your ally, instead of your enemy. Be sure to write it from the viewpoint of being in your top three favorite states. Assume that if they can provide what you ask for, they will.

I love you, and I trust you to have my best interests at heart, and it brings me so much joy to be friends. Laughing till we cry is the highlight of my month. I value my privacy and choose to share certain details with only a few people. It makes me feel I have a special relationship with those who know the private details of my life. And I like to have respect that comes from not having everyone know all the mistakes I've made. Would you help me with this?

EXERCISE—Strategy

1. First, write down a Hot Potato.
2. Answer these questions:
   - What is it you want to "have" in your relationship with that person? There are two definitions of *have*, one means to "possess," and the other is to "experience." Since you never actually possess the other person in a relationship, the only way to "have" a relationship is to "experience" it.
   - How are you trying to change them?
   - What ideals of theirs are unacceptable to you?
   - What are you worried they will take away from you?
   - How do you worry they will try to make you behave in a way that is contrary to your ideals?
   - What do you think they will try to take away that is scarce and needed for you to survive and thrive? Is it really scarce?

3. After writing this all down, it is helpful to take several deep breaths and let these questions settle.

4. The next step is to simply write out what it would be like to say exactly what you want and why, as though that other person were **totally and completely** on board as your ally, instead of your enemy. Be sure to write it from the viewpoint of being in your top three states. Assume that if they can provide that for you, they will.

If you do this in the future, you will be communicating honestly and purely and with no manipulation. We are so afraid of a "no," just like that salesman in Chapter 10, or a confrontation, an awkward situation, or a potential argument, we develop an entire arsenal of strategies, tactics, and deception, rather than bare our souls and speak from our heart.

29

A MORE
MESSY MESS

There is one final thing to look at. What makes this MESS even more MESSY? It is the "Y"—it's YOU. Not in a "There's something wrong with you" way, but simply your mental relationship with yourself.

In the book *The Four Sacred Secrets*, the authors Preethaji and Krishnaji say, "The root cause of suffering is obsessive self-centric thinking."

Just to be clear, obsessive self-centric thinking is not self-love or self-compassion. You can't have enough of those two. It is self-centric THINKING. There is a mental mechanism that keeps every thought focused on I, me, mine, and my.

Take any upsetting thought you have, and now take YOU out of it. It's so crazy yet 100% effective.

Let's take an example, "My father ignored me when I told him I needed to talk to him about something important. OUCH!" Would something like that hurt? Can you feel it?

What if you took YOU out of it. It would be along the lines of, "The biological child of a person indicated a need to talk, and the biological parent did something else besides acknowledging that person's need." Can you see the difference? Without YOU in it, there is less hurt. Perhaps there is more compassion for all the people involved or a desire for a loving solution without as much judgment.

As with everything we have looked at, there are some really positive things about all our thoughts being all about us.

Why It's Awesome

What's great about obsessive self-centric thinking? As living organisms, we have a built-in survival mechanism, which is essential because otherwise, well, we wouldn't survive. Just like the earlier examples of heights creating tension and making us back away from the ledge, this is incredibly useful and can be lifesaving.

However, our thoughts mirror and create a running narrative about what is happening: "I must move away from the ledge, or I will die." It's sort of like having a sports announcer always in your head...but one this is obsessive about only one team—YOU.

Why It's Not

There is so much freedom from suffering available if you look at situations from other viewpoints. Arguments can be entertaining, fear exhilarating, and sorrow can be achingly beautiful when we take a step back.

For the last exercise, we are going to practice taking YOU out of the equation.

Preparing You for The Exercise

First, you'll be using a Hot Potato you have cooled down, it will help to write it down.

For example: *My husband told me he wanted a divorce. OUCH!*

1. You will rewrite this by taking yourself, or any reference to yourself, out of the sentence.

    A man said to a person he had a legal contract with, that he wanted to end the legal contract.

Or perhaps:

A man said to a person he had expressed affection towards in the past, that he no longer wanted to express affection.

2. You will write down how an alien from another planet might view this.

    A creature with four appendages had sounds come out of its head, and the second creature seemed surprised and upset.

3. You will write how the other person, from their own obsessively self-centric view, would see this.

    Husband's viewpoint: "I couldn't take it anymore. I was so unhappy in the marriage that I had to make a change to make my life better."

4. You will write out how you would view this from each of your three favorite states. For the sake of this example, I'll use compassion, curiosity, and trust.

First Favorite State—***Compassion:***

There was so much suffering happening in the relationship, and this created more. What help could comfort them?

Second Favorite State—***Curiosity:***

There is so much to experience about how this feels for each person; I should learn more.

Third Favorite State—***Trust:***

Each person is doing the best they can. It will all work out for the best.

5. This is going to give you a wide variety of different perspectives to look at this from. Select which of these feels best to you—which one creates the least hurt and the most connection.

EXERCISE—It's Not About You

Find a Hot Potato you have cooled down.

1. Write it down.
2. Now rewrite this event, but this time take yourself or any reference to yourself, out of the sentence.
3. Write how an alien from another planet might view this.
4. Write how the other person, from their own obsessively self-centric view, would see this.
5. Write out how you would view this from each of your three favorite states.

First Favorite State—_____
The event would now be:

Second Favorite State—_____
The event would now be:

Third Favorite State _____
The event would now be:

6. Select which of them feels best to you—which of the three creates the least hurt and the most connection.

Feeling it is all about you is like being Atlas, bent over from carrying the weight of the world on your shoulders. If you can stop this, you will be able to stand tall again.

30

ARRIVALS AND DEPARTURES

You may ask, "So now what's next? What should I DO?"

Other than the exercises, there are no rules or even guidelines about what to DO. What *the Power of OUCH!* has given you, is an opportunity to reevaluate what state you want to be in and what you want to have going forward.

The way you behave will start to automatically change now that we've drawn your attention to certain thoughts, meanings, reactions, and patterns.

Speaking of which, "behave" is an interesting word. It means, "act or conduct oneself in a specified way, especially toward others." I believe if we place our attention on the BE part—consciously choose how we are being, and what state we are being in—and clearly define the HAVE part—consciously choose the experiences we want—then the BEHAVING will take care of itself.

Notice if that is true, and let me know how *The Power of OUCH!* has helped your being and having—because you deserve to BE and HAVE everything you want.

As I told you in the first chapter, I've written this book because I truly believe that this will help you create better connections in your life. As your Tour Guide, I want to thank you for choosing to come on this journey, down this path, through the overgrown jungle, and out into the clearing with me.

I hope you have enjoyed the explorations on our trip, and I truly hope you didn't experience too many figurative bumps, bruises, or mosquito bites. But, as opposed to most Tour Guides, I sincerely hope you lost some baggage—emotional baggage, that is—along the way.

ABOUT THE AUTHOR

After experiencing decades of hurt and disappointment in her long-term romantic relationships, Sondra set off to discover why she kept running into the same painful problem with her relationships. She's worked with renowned relationship experts in the US and studied under mystic sages in India, becoming a certified meditation teacher, a transformational relationship coach, and author.

Sondra is on a mission to help people heal from the hurt, disrespect, and disappointment experienced in any close relationship so they can stay connected and continue creating the joy, connection, and intimacy that makes great relationships priceless.

She lives in Puerto Rico enjoying life with her much-loved husband, where she writes, leads workshops and hosts retreats. You can find her online at sondraharmon. com to get access to her social channels and learn where she will be speaking, or you can always write to her at me@sondraharmon.com.

Sweep it Under the Rug

Blame

Self-Blame

Run

Hide

Reasons & Rules

Numb & Distract

Daydream & Hope

179

Offerings & Sacrifices

File

Enlist

Rewind & Replay

Made in the USA
Monee, IL
24 February 2021